The 17-Day DREAM BLUEPRINT

The 17-Day DREAM BLUEPRINT

Transforming Your Dreams into Reality

DR. DONDI M. DAY

Emerald Isle Publishing

The 17-Day Dream Blueprint: Transforming Your Dreams into Reality

Library of Congress Cataloging-in-Publication Data has been applied for and is on record at the Library of Congress.

Copyright © 2024 by Dr. Dondi M. Day

All rights reserved.

ISBN: 979-8-218-45669-6 (Hardback)

No part of this publication may be reproduced, distributed, or transmitted in any form or by any means, including photocopying, recording, or other electronic or mechanical methods, without the prior written permission of the author, except in the case of brief quotations embodied in critical reviews and certain other noncommercial uses permitted by copyright law. The stories, all names, characters, and incidents portrayed in this book are fictitious. Any resemblance to actual persons, living or dead, is purely coincidental.

Quotes attributed to other authors and individuals within this publication are believed to be in the public domain and are not claimed as original content by the author of this work.

Published by Emerald Isle Publishing, Inc.
PO Box 5041
Emerald Isle, NC 28594

dondi.day@emeraldislepublishing.com

DEDICATION AND ACKNOWLEDGEMENTS

*To my guiding light, Almighty God,
my loving wife, Tracey,
and our precious boys, Brayden and Logan—this book is for you.*

To the reader, I hope this book inspires you to chase your DREAMS.

With heartfelt gratitude to Dr. Gerald and the esteemed faculty at Liberty University, whose collective mentorship and unwavering encouragement made this journey not only possible but also profoundly enriching.

I would like to express my heartfelt gratitude to Lt. Col. Brad Creedon, whose unwavering guidance and support were instrumental in the creation of this book. Your invaluable insights and encouragement have truly made a significant impact on my journey.

CONTENTS

Introduction 1

PART I: D—DEFINE YOUR DREAMS 3

Day 1: The Journey Toward Achieving Our Dreams 5

   The Unpredictable Path to Our Dreams 6
   Internal Barriers to Our Dreams 7
   Whispers of the Unlived Life 9
   Seeds of a Scientist: Nurturing Passion Amidst Doubt 10
   From Whispers to Reality: Awakening Your Dreams 12
   The Journey Begins With a Single Step 12
   Conclusion 16

Day 2: From Dream to Destination 19

   ACTDRIVE (Action, Celebrate, Adjust, Visualize, Recognize, Ignore, Value, Empower) 19
   Self-Discovery 21
   Charting Your Course: SMART Goals and Objectives 24
   Why SMART Goals Work 25
   Crafting Your SMART Goals 25
   Objectives: Your Roadmap to Success 27
   Harnessing Visual Tools for Effective Goal Setting 27
      Mind Maps 27
   Turning Your Dreams into Reality 28
   Sarah's Bookstore Dream: Taking the First Step 30
   Conclusion 33

PART II: R - REIMAGINE YOUR POSSIBILITIES 35

Day 3: The Science Behind Self-Motivation 37
What is self-motivation? 37
The Anatomy of Self-Motivation 38
The Neurochemical Symphony of Motivation 39
The Psychology of Motivation 40
Environmental Influences 40
The Peak of John's Ambition: A Mount Rainier Ascent 41
Conclusion 43

Day 4: Fueling Your Fire: Intrinsic vs. Extrinsic Motivation 47
Intrinsic Motivation: The Joy of the Journey 47
Extrinsic Motivation: The Lure of Rewards 48
The Synergy of Intrinsic and Extrinsic Motivation 49
The Potential Pitfalls of Over-Reliance on Extrinsic Motivation 49
Striking a Balance 50
Finding Your Inner Drive 50
Liam's Music Passion: Finding Joy Beyond Rewards 56
Rediscovering the Joy 56
A New Perspective 57
Building a Community 57
Conclusion 58

Day 5: Igniting the Engine: Building Self-Efficacy for Lasting Motivation .. 61
The Four Pillars of Self-Efficacy 62
Building Your Self-Efficacy Muscle 62
Fanning the Flames: Finding Your Passion and Igniting Purpose 63
Unleashing Your Inner Explorer 64
The Transformative Power of Passion 67
Rachel's Public Speaking Breakthrough: Building Confidence Step by Step 67
The First Step 68
Taking the Stage 69
Building Momentum 69
Reflecting on the Journey 70
Conclusion 70

Day 6: Tapping into Peak Performance and Intrinsic Joy 73
The Benefits of Flow 74
How to Find Your Flow 75
Savoring Success: Celebrating Milestones and Cultivating Gratitude 76

The Power of Celebration...76
Cultivating Gratitude...77
Chris's Artistic Flow: Finding Joy in the Creative Process 82
 Reconnecting with the Process...*82*
 Finding Flow..*83*
 Sharing the Joy..*83*
Conclusion 84

Day 7: Igniting Your Professional Passion and Achieving Career Goals 89

Mark's Career Pivot: Finding Purpose in Professional Passion.....................96
 Exploring New Paths..*97*
 Finding a Mentor *97*
 Taking the Leap *98*
Conclusion 99

PART III: E - EMBRACE CHALLENGES AS OPPORTUNITIES 101

Day 8: Roadblocks to Resolve 103

Internal Motivation Killers...103
External Motivation Killers..109
Anna's Fitness Routine: Small Habits, Big Changes....................................121
 Setting Small Goals..*122*
 Building Momentum *122*
 Adding to the Routine *122*
 Embracing the Changes *123*
Conclusion 124

Day 9: Overcoming Obstacles to Stay Motivated 127

Embracing the Inevitable: Obstacles as Opportunities 127
Time Management Strategies 128
The Power of Action 128
Mastering Time Management 128
Strategies for Overcoming Obstacles 129
Overcoming Procrastination and Self-Doubt 130
Navigating the Storm: Strategies for Overcoming Obstacles.......................132
Maya's Entrepreneurial Journey: Turning Setbacks into Comebacks 135
 The First Setback *136*
 The Product Delay *136*
 Turning Setbacks into Comebacks *137*
Conclusion 138

PART IV: A - ASSEMBLE YOUR SUPPORT NETWORK 139

Day 10: Strengthening Relationships through Self-Motivation 141

Nurturing Connections: Strategies for Building Stronger Bonds 141
Self-Motivation's Ripple Effect 143
Elena's Connection Quest: Building Stronger Bonds 143
- *Taking Small Steps* *144*
- *Building Workplace Relationships* *144*
- *Rekindling Friendships* *145*
- *Creating Deeper Connections* *145*

Conclusion 146

Day 11: Cultivating Self-Motivation for Effective Leadership 149

The Motivated Leader: Qualities and Characteristics 149
Leading at Work 151
Leading at School 152
Leading at Home 152
Leading with Purpose: A Lifelong Journey 154
Carlos's Leadership Journey: Inspiring Others Through Self-Motivation 156
- *Reigniting Self-Motivation* *156*
- *Connecting with the Team* *157*
- *Leading by Example* *157*
- *Encouraging Collaboration and Innovation* *158*
- *Reflection* *158*

Conclusion 158

PART V: M - MAP OUT YOUR PATH 161

Day 12: Cultivating Your Oasis 163

Creating Your Personal Haven 164
Jake's Home Office Transformation: Creating a Space for Success 168
- *Assessing the Current Setup* *168*
- *Decluttering and Organizing* *169*
- *Optimizing the Layout* *169*
- *Adding Personal Touches* *170*
- *Final Touches* *170*

Conclusion 171

Day 13: Harnessing the Power of Habit for Lasting Motivation 173
    The Science of Habit Formation 174
    Breaking the Chains: Michael's Journey to Freedom from Smoking 174
    Harnessing the Power of Habit for Motivation........................... 176
    Conclusion 179

PART VI: S - SUSTAIN MOMENTUM THROUGH SETBACKS 181

Day 14: Self-Motivation as the Catalyst 183
    Embracing Lifelong Learning.. 183
    Expanding Your Horizons 187
    The Transformative Power of Self-Motivation 189
    Raj's Ironman Training: Staying Motivated for the Long Haul 191
        Finding New Motivation.. 191
        Overcoming Setbacks.. 192
        Staying Mentally Strong 192
        Race Day... 193
    Conclusion 194

Day 15: Embracing Life's Challenges 197
    Life's Journey 197
    The Power of Writing Down Your Fears 198
    Reframing Your Thoughts and Fears 200
    Sophia's Dual Passions: Balancing Career and Hobbies 201
        Creating a Balanced Routine 201
        Setting Boundaries and Prioritizing..................................... 202
        Finding Joy in the Process 202
        Integrating Passions into Daily Life 203
    Conclusion 203

Day 16: Showing Gratitude and Positive Affirmations 207
    Building a Support System and Cultivating Self-Motivation 208
    The Power of Intention 209
    Affirmations.. 211
    John's Gratitude Practice: Transforming Life with Positive Affirmations 212
        Starting a Gratitude Practice 213
        Finding the Positives 213
        Deepening the Practice 214
        Overcoming Challenges 214
    Conclusion 214

Day 17: Embracing Your Power: A New Chapter of Self-Motivation............217
   Interactive Reflection 217
   Reflecting on Your Journey of Self-Motivation 218
   Your Next Steps on the Journey 218
   Conclusion and Introduction to Lifelong Learning 219
   Final Conclusion and Looking Ahead 219

Bibliography...223

Index..227

Let's Stay in Touch! 231

About the Author..232

Additional Published Works 233

"The future belongs to those
who believe in the beauty of their dreams."

—Eleanor Roosevelt

INTRODUCTION

Have you ever felt the weight of an unfulfilled dream, a yearning for something more, yet found yourself frozen in a state of inaction? You're not alone. Millions share this struggle, held back by self-doubt and the perceived enormity of the task ahead. Whether it's Anna, who dreams of starting her own business, or Raj, who wishes to participate in the IRONMAN triathlon, fear and procrastination often keep these dreams confined to their imaginations.

Consider the words of legendary mountaineer Ed Viesturs, who has stood atop the world's highest peaks 21 times: "You never conquer the mountain. You conquer yourself—your doubts and fears." This truth transcends mountaineering and speaks to human potential—your potential!

It's a reminder that the most formidable obstacles often lie within us. But what if you had a guide—a roadmap—to navigate these internal barriers and unlock the motivation that lies dormant within you?

That's where "The 17-Day Dream Blueprint: Transforming Your Dreams into Reality" comes in. Within these pages, you'll discover a unique, actionable framework—the **DREAMS** Method—designed to propel you from inaction to achievement:

- **D**efine your dreams and aspirations.
- **R**eimagine your possibilities.
- **E**mbrace challenges as opportunities.
- **A**ssemble your support network
- **M**ap out your path.
- **S**ustain momentum through setbacks

Unlike other books on motivation, "The 17-Day Dream Blueprint" goes beyond theory, offering tangible tools and practical exercises grounded in psychological research to identify your deepest desires, set meaningful goals, and create a personalized action plan. It teaches you how to cultivate resilience, overcome self-doubt, and tap into the unwavering determination that resides within you.

This book is designed as a 17-day journey, with each day dedicated to completing specific tasks. Start by jotting down your biggest dream as you approach Day 1, engaging immediately with the transformative process. Take your time to read, reflect, and answer the thought-provoking questions provided. However, if you're feeling ambitious, you can complete the entire journey in less time. Ultimately, the pace is yours to choose, ensuring a personalized and impactful experience.

Don't let another day pass you by. Unlock your potential by embracing this chance to embark on a transformative journey of self-exploration and growth. Break free from the chains of procrastination and self-doubt and unlock the extraordinary potential that lies within you. This book is your compass, your roadmap to living a life on your terms.

Your dreams are waiting. Are you ready to take that first step with "The 17-Day Dream Blueprint"?

PART I:

D—DEFINE YOUR DREAMS

> "A journey of a thousand miles begins with a single step."
>
> —Lao Tzu

DAY 1:
THE JOURNEY TOWARD ACHIEVING OUR DREAMS

Welcome to Day 1 of your transformative journey with "The 17-Day Dream Blueprint." Today marks the beginning of a powerful shift—from passively dreaming to actively pursuing your deepest desires and aspirations. Imagine the path to your dreams as a scenic route, not a straight highway. There will be unexpected turns, breathtaking vistas, and challenging climbs, but the rewards at the summit are worth every step. Life's curveballs may test your resolve, but remember, these obstacles are not roadblocks; they are stepping-stones designed to propel you towards your true potential.

While external challenges like unexpected setbacks or limited resources can seem daunting, it's the internal barriers that often pose the greatest threat to our progress. Think of those moments when you felt the spark of a dream, a vision of a brighter future, yet hesitated to take that first step. Fear of failure, uncertainty, or the nagging voice of self-doubt may have whispered in your ear, urging you to stay in your comfort zone. We've all encountered those moments of doubt and indecision. But what if I told you that within these moments of hesitation lies the key to unlocking extraordinary possibilities?

Instead of viewing these internal obstacles as limitations, let's reframe them as opportunities for growth and transformation. In this chapter, we'll embark on a profound journey of self-discovery, exploring the intricate landscape of your dreams and aspirations. We'll delve deep into your desires, confront your fears head-on, and unearth the untapped potential that lies dormant within you. By understanding the unique challenges you face and learning to navigate them with confidence, you can turn your dreams into a vibrant reality.

So, take a deep breath and embrace this journey with an open heart and a curious mind. Together, we'll uncover the tools, strategies, and mindset shifts that will empower you to overcome obstacles, ignite your motivation, and create a life that truly reflects your dreams. Welcome to the beginning of an extraordinary adventure—your dream journey awaits!

The Unpredictable Path to Our Dreams

The journey to achieving our dreams is rarely a smooth, linear one. It's more akin to navigating the vast and unpredictable ocean, where calm seas can quickly transform into turbulent storms. Life, much like the ocean's currents, can change course unexpectedly. Unforeseen events, such as unplanned pregnancies, sudden illnesses, or financial crises, can act as rogue waves, tossing us off our charted path and forcing us to re-evaluate our priorities and adjust our sails. These external challenges can be overwhelming, but they also offer opportunities for growth, resilience, and the discovery of hidden strengths within us.

However, navigating these challenges requires more than just weathering external storms. It also demands a deep understanding of ourselves, our motivations, and the underlying fears that may hold us back. It's a voyage of self-discovery and introspection, where we learn to chart the depths of our own inner compass and harness the courage and resilience needed to stay the course, even when the waters are rough.

Take a moment to reflect on a time in your life when an unexpected event altered your path. How did you adapt? What did you learn from the experience? By examining these turning points, we can gain valuable insights into our own strengths and weaknesses, ultimately equipping us to navigate future challenges with greater confidence and clarity.

Internal Barriers to Our Dreams

The journey to realizing our dreams is not only about navigating external challenges; it's also about confronting the internal barriers that can hold us back. By recognizing and understanding these obstacles, we can begin to dismantle them, freeing ourselves to pursue our passions with greater confidence and clarity. This is the essence of the transformative journey we're embarking on together.

Our natural inclination towards comfort and familiarity can create resistance to change. We crave stability and routine, making it difficult to embrace the unknown and step outside our comfort zones to achieve our dreams[1]. This resistance can hinder personal growth, prevent us from seizing new opportunities, and lead to stagnation or regret. It's like having a map to hidden treasure but being too afraid to leave the familiar path.

To illustrate, I've experienced this firsthand. Despite my best intentions, the home gym I assembled during the pandemic sits unused. This inertia, the gap between intention and action, is a common struggle. Researchers suggest that this resistance to change is deeply rooted in our psychology[2].

Fear of failure can be paralyzing. We might become preoccupied with what-if scenarios, imagining all the ways our endeavors could go wrong.

---

1 Anita Dyb Linge et al., "Bandura's Self-Efficacy Model Used to Explore Participants' Experiences of Health, Lifestyle, and Work After Attending a Vocational Rehabilitation Program with Lifestyle Intervention – a Focus Group Study," *Journal of Multidisciplinary Healthcare* Volume 14 (2021), https://doi.org/10.2147/jmdh.s334620.
2 Lucas Carden and Wendy Wood, "Habit Formation and Change," *Current Opinion in Behavioral Sciences* 20 (2018), https://doi.org/10.1016/j.cobeha.2017.12.009.

This can manifest as procrastination, perfectionism, or even self-sabotage, as we unconsciously avoid failure by never truly starting or by setting ourselves up for disappointment. Psychologists like Carol Dweck, known for her work on the "growth mindset," emphasize that viewing challenges as opportunities for growth rather than threats can help overcome the fear of failure. The key to overcoming this fear is to reframe failure as a learning opportunity, a steppingstone towards success, rather than a final end.

Similarly, fear of judgment can hold us back. We may worry about what others think of our choices, abilities, or dreams. This fear can lead to self-censorship, where we stifle our creative expression or hide our true selves out of fear of ridicule or rejection. To overcome this fear, we need to cultivate self-acceptance and recognize that not everyone will understand or appreciate our journey. The opinions of others should not dictate our path!

In a similar vein, I've seen this struggle in others as well. A childhood friend, whom I'll call Laura, confided in me about an unpublished book she had written. Her fear of judgment or ridicule prevented her from sharing her work with the world. This story highlights how creative potential often lies dormant, waiting for the courage to overcome self-doubt and embrace change.

Laura's unspoken story, her creative potential locked away due to fear, struck a chord deep within me. I saw my own fears and insecurities reflected back at me. It made me realize that I wasn't alone in my struggle to overcome self-doubt and share my passions with the world. This realization sparked a desire to explore my own buried dreams and aspirations.

Whispers of the Unlived Life

These individual struggles are echoed on a larger scale. Les Brown, a motivational speaker, once said[3]:

> The graveyard is the richest place on earth because it is here that you will find all the hopes and dreams that were never fulfilled, the books that were never written, the songs that were never sung, the inventions that were never shared, and the cures that were never discovered, all because someone was too afraid to take that first step, keep with the problem, or be determined to carry out their dreams.

His words paint a vivid picture of the graveyard's untapped potential, a reminder of the countless dreams and aspirations that wither away due to fear, procrastination, or a lack of determination.

When I first heard Brown's message, it was as if he was speaking directly to my soul. I was grappling with my own inner struggles, and his words served as a spark, igniting a renewed sense of purpose and a strong desire to create a better future for my family. The desire to give my children a better life became my driving force. This realization not only fueled my personal journey but also shed light on a universal challenge: the fear of judgment.

The fear of judgment and ridicule can be a powerful deterrent, often looming largest on the precipice of success. To overcome this, it's essential to cultivate a mindset of resilience and self-acceptance. Embrace feedback as a tool for growth, and remember that not everyone's opinion reflects your worth or potential. My friend Laura's unpublished book is a testament to this struggle. Countless aspiring authors, artists, creators, and entrepreneurs hesitate at this crucial moment, their brilliance hidden within unopened books, unsung melodies, and unshared inventions.

---

3   Les Brown, "The Graveyard Is the Richest Place on Earth.," accessed June 6, 2024, https://www.youtube.com/watch?v=YgjNfn8nlj8.

Reflection: What internal barriers have held you back from pursuing your dreams? How can you reframe these obstacles into opportunities for growth and transformation?

_____

_____

_____

_____

Seeds of a Scientist: Nurturing Passion Amidst Doubt

Emily stood at the edge of the bustling science fair, her heart pounding. Her project, meticulously crafted to illustrate the dire effects of ocean acidification, drew curious glances. But with the judges' arrival imminent, her confidence wavered.

Sensing her anxiety, Mrs. Parker, her science teacher and mentor, approached with a warm smile. "Feeling nervous, Emily?"

Emily nodded; eyes glued to her neatly arranged pamphlets. "What if I stumble over my words? What if they think my project is insignificant?"

Mrs. Parker chuckled softly, her calm demeanor radiating reassurance. "Emily, remember, every great scientist started as a student filled with questions and prone to mistakes. It's not about having all the answers; it's about your eagerness to learn and the courage to voice your curiosity."

"But what if I fail?" Emily whispered; her voice barely audible.

"Then you learn," Mrs. Parker replied gently. "Failure is merely a steppingstone, not a dead end. Tell me, what's at the heart of your project? Why does it matter so deeply to you?"

Emily inhaled, her thoughts focusing on the countless hours dedicated to research. "Our oceans are becoming more acidic, harming marine life... it breaks my heart. If we don't understand this, how can we protect them?"

Mrs. Parker's eyes sparkled. "There it is, Emily! Your passion for the ocean is your greatest strength. Let that passion fuel your presentation. Speak from the heart, and you'll connect with your audience. Let them see why this matters to you."

A flicker of confidence ignited within Emily. "Okay," she nodded, "I can do that. Thank you, Mrs. Parker."

As the judges approached, Emily stood taller, her nerves settling. With newfound conviction, she greeted them, "Welcome to my project on ocean acidification. Let's explore why this is crucial, not just for marine life, but for all of us."

Mrs. Parker watched with pride as Emily eloquently explained her research, her earlier fears replaced by the power of her own words.

Afterward, Mrs. Parker joined her, her eyes beaming. "You were brilliant, Emily. How do you feel?"

A radiant smile spread across Emily's face. "Amazing! They were so engaged, asked great questions, and I actually knew the answers!"

"Of course you did," Mrs. Parker affirmed. "You were prepared, and your passion shone through. Remember this feeling, Emily? It's proof that you're capable of far more than you realize."

Years later, Emily stood on the deck of a research vessel, gazing out at the vast expanse of the ocean. Beside her stood a young intern, her face etched with worry about her upcoming deep-sea dive.

Echoing Mrs. Parker's words, Emily placed a reassuring hand on her shoulder. "Feeling nervous?"

The intern nodded, her grip tightening on the railing.

"Remember why you're here," Emily encouraged. "Let your love for the ocean guide you. Dive into your fears, and you'll discover they aren't as deep as you think."

Inspired by her mentor's calm resolve, the intern met Emily's gaze. "Thank you, Emily. I'll keep that in mind."

As the boat gently swayed with the waves, Emily smiled, knowing she had passed on the torch of encouragement, a beacon of hope for the next generation of ocean advocates.

From Whispers to Reality: Awakening Your Dreams

Turning a dream into reality is a dynamic and multifaceted process that involves a combination of self-reflection, planning, and action. It begins with identifying and clarifying your dream, understanding what it truly means to you, and why it holds significance in your life. This involves introspection and soul-searching to uncover the underlying motivations and desires that fuel your aspirations.

What dreams have you buried deep down? Perhaps there's a novel waiting to be written, a business to be started, a song yearning to be sung, or a painting longing to be shared with the world. Whatever it is, I hope you find the courage to unearth it and let it shine. Let this book serve as your guide. It's time to silence the whispers of the unlived life and embark on a transformative journey. Let's take that first step together.

The Journey Begins With a Single Step

Take a few moments to reflect on your own dreams and aspirations. What are those hidden desires that you've been hesitant to pursue? Remember, this isn't about creating a to-do list; it's about connecting with your deepest passions and allowing them to guide your path. Embrace this exercise as a crucial step towards unlocking your full potential and living a life that truly reflects your dreams. Here are a few of mine:

- *Creative Expression*:
  - o Write and publish more books: Continue to develop my writing skills and share my stories with the world.
  - o Explore other forms of creative expression: Experiment with music to unlock new avenues of creativity.
  - o Build a platform: Establish a strong online presence to share my work and connect with fellow creatives.
- *Global Exploration*:
  - o Travel to at least 10 countries: Immerse myself in different cultures, learn new languages, and broaden my perspectives.
  - o Volunteer abroad: Contribute my time and skills to meaningful projects that make a difference in the lives of others.
  - o Document my travels: Share my experiences through writing, photography, and videography to inspire others to explore the world.
- *Meaningful Contribution to Society*:
  - o Start a foundation: Establish a non-profit organization focused on empowering children through music, education, and mentorship.
  - o Mentor young writers: Share my knowledge and experience to help aspiring authors find their voice and achieve their dreams.
  - o Advocate for social justice: Use my platform to raise awareness and support causes that promote equality and opportunity for all.

These are just a few examples of my own personal dreams and aspirations. Take a moment to reflect on your own desires. What whispers of an unlived life echo within you? Is it starting a business that solves a problem you're passionate about? Perhaps it's traveling the world. Maybe it's taking that art class you've always wanted to try. Now is the time to unearth those dreams and give them a chance to blossom. Embrace this exercise as a first step towards unlocking your full potential and living a life that reflects your passions and dreams.

Don't let fear hold you back. The world is waiting for your brilliance to shine.

Use this white space to list your dreams and aspirations:

Exercise: Choose one dream from your list and write a short paragraph about what it would mean to you to achieve it.

Conclusion

Today, we've explored the winding path to our dreams, recognizing the external and internal challenges that can hinder our progress. We've seen how our comfort zones and fears can hold us back, but we've also been reminded that every journey begins with a single step.

As you reflect on your own dreams and aspirations, remember the stories of Laura and Emily. Their experiences remind us that fear and self-doubt are common obstacles, but they can be overcome. By confronting those fears, setting SMART goals, and taking that first small step, you can begin to transform your dreams into reality.

Remember, this is your journey. It's okay to feel uncertain or overwhelmed. But with each small step you take, you'll gain confidence, clarity, and momentum.

Tomorrow, we'll dive deeper into the ACTDRIVE method, a powerful framework designed to help you take action and stay motivated on your journey. We'll explore how to set SMART goals, break them down into manageable objectives, and create a personalized roadmap to success.

Get ready to turn your dreams into actionable plans and start living the life you've always imagined. The journey continues, and I can't wait to see what you achieve!

Notes

"What you get by achieving your goals is not as important as what you become by achieving your goals."

—Zig Ziglar

DAY 2:
FROM DREAM TO DESTINATION

In the previous chapter, we embarked on a journey of self-discovery, unearthing our deepest dreams and aspirations. We learned that these desires are not mere fantasies but the seeds of our potential, waiting to be nurtured and transformed into reality. Today, we'll take the next step in this transformative journey by turning those dreams into actionable goals.

Dreams and aspirations are the seeds of potential—the whispers from our hearts that ignite our passions. They are the "what ifs" and "maybes" that dance in our imaginations, beckoning us towards a future filled with purpose and fulfillment. But how do we bridge the gap between these dreams and reality?

Get ready to embark on a transformative journey. We'll delve into the art of turning those dreams into tangible, achievable goals. Consider this book your guide, your map, and your compass as you navigate this exciting voyage from dream to destination. Remember, you are not alone on this path. I'll be by your side, offering support and encouragement every step of the way. Let's transform your dreams from whispers into reality!

ACTDRIVE
(Action, Celebrate, Adjust, Visualize, Recognize, Ignore, Value, Empower)

Before we start outlining your goals, there are a few important things you must internalize. These principles, which we'll call the ACTDRIVE method, are crucial for taking action and being driven toward your goals.

1. **Action.** Embarking on a new journey often feels like the most daunting part, echoing Stephen King's words: "The scariest moment is always just

before you start." It's the leap into the unknown, where dreams shift from ethereal wisps to tangible actions. However, as Martin Luther King Jr. wisely advised, "You don't have to see the whole staircase, just take the first step." That initial action sparks momentum, dissipates doubts, and ignites a transformative chain reaction.

2. **Celebrate Milestones.** As you progress towards your goals, acknowledging and celebrating your achievements along the way reinforces your progress and fuels your motivation to continue. Paulo Coelho eloquently said, "The great victory, which appears so simple today, was the result of a series of small victories that went unnoticed."

3. **Adapt and Adjust Your Sails.** Life is unpredictable, and so is the path to your goals. Embracing adaptability is key; as motivational speaker Tony Robbins wisely advises, "Stay committed to your decisions, but stay flexible in your approach." Rather than being discouraged by setbacks, view them as valuable opportunities to learn, grow, and refine your strategies. Remember, the most successful journeys often involve unexpected detours and recalibrations.

4. **Visualize Your Success.** Visualization is a powerful tool that can significantly impact your journey toward achieving your goals. Take time each day to imagine yourself having already achieved your dreams and aspirations. As Eleanor Roosevelt eloquently stated, "The future belongs to those who believe in the beauty of their dreams."

5. **Recognize That Personal Change Can Be Hard.** Change is rarely easy. Acknowledge the difficulty of personal change and accept that there will be setbacks and challenges. Don't beat yourself up if you stumble or falter. Remember, progress—not perfection—is the goal. Edison once said, "I didn't fail 1,000 times. The light bulb was an invention with 1,000 steps."

6. **Ignore the Haters and Detractors.** On your journey, you're bound to encounter naysayers and critics who, as Mary Kay Ash once said, "Aerodynamically, the bumblebee shouldn't be able to fly, but the bumblebee

doesn't know it, so it goes on flying anyway." Don't allow their doubts to become your own. Instead, use their negativity as fuel to propel you forward, proving them wrong through your actions and achievements. Embrace Ash's empowering reminder that "Many people limit themselves to what they think they can do. You can go as far as your mind lets you. What you believe, remember, you can achieve." Don't let self-imposed limitations hold you back; trust in your abilities and strive for the extraordinary.

7. **Lose the Victim Mentality.** Shedding the victim mentality is a transformative journey to reclaim personal power and autonomy. As Matthew McConaughey aptly stated, "Life's not fair. It never was, isn't now, and it won't ever be. Do not fall into the entitlement trap of feeling like you're a victim. You are not." Embrace this truth by shifting from feeling powerless to recognizing your ability to shape your own destiny. Change any negative thoughts, let go of blame and resentment, and replace self-defeating thoughts with affirmations like "I am capable," "I am worthy of success," and "I can achieve anything I set my mind to."

Self-Discovery

As Aristotle wisely said, "Knowing yourself is the beginning of all wisdom." Our journey begins with introspection and self-discovery, revisiting those dreams and aspirations you captured on Day 1. Take a deep breath, turn inward, and allow your true desires to surface. Reflect on what truly makes your heart sing, the activities that ignite your soul, and the impact you wish to make on the world. By uncovering your values, passions, and aspirations, you will lay the foundation upon which your goals will be built. Once you have a clear vision of your desired future, we will break down those grand aspirations into smaller, more manageable steps.

Now, grab your favorite pen, find a quiet space, and begin this transformative journey of self-discovery.

1. What dreams do you hold in the deepest recesses of your heart?

_____

_____

_____

2. What truly makes your heart sing?

_____

_____

_____

3. What activities make you feel alive and energized?

_____

_____

_____

_____

4. What are your unique talents and strengths?

_____

_____

_____

_____

5. What kind of impact do you want to have on the world?

_____

_____

_____

_____

6. Do you long for a life filled with laughter and love, adventure and excitement, or perhaps peace and tranquility?

_____

_____

_____

_____

Congratulations on taking this important step! By answering these questions, you have begun to unveil the depths of your being. As you move forward, remember that the journey of self-discovery is ongoing. Embrace the process, be open to new insights, and allow your dreams to guide you toward a fulfilling and purposeful life.

Charting Your Course: SMART Goals and Objectives

As Carl Jung wisely said, "Until you make the unconscious conscious, it will direct your life and you will call it fate." To take control of our destiny, we must first become aware of our desires and then translate them into actionable plans.

Imagine embarking on a road trip without a map or GPS. You might have a general idea of where you want to go, but without a clear route, you're likely to get lost, waste time, and feel frustrated. This same principle applies to our goals in life.

Without a clear destination and a well-defined path to get there, we can easily lose motivation and direction. That's where SMART goals come in. These act as steppingstones, guiding us towards our ultimate vision and providing a sense of progress and accomplishment along the way.

SMART[4] is an acronym that stands for:

- **Specific**: Clearly define your goal. What exactly do you want to achieve? Avoid vague or general statements like "I want to be healthier" or "I want to be more successful." Instead, be specific: "I want to lose 10 pounds" or "I want to get a promotion at work."
- **Measurable**: How will you know when you've reached your goal? Establish concrete criteria for measuring progress. This could be a number (e.g., weight loss, income increase), a deadline (e.g., finish a project by a certain date), or a specific outcome (e.g., run a marathon).
- **Achievable**: Your goal should be challenging but realistic. Setting realistic goals is key to staying motivated and avoiding frustration. Take into account your available resources, skillset, and time constraints when defining your objectives.

---

4 May Britt Bjerke and Ralph Renger, "Being Smart About Writing Smart Objectives," *Evaluation and Program Planning* 61 (2017), https://doi.org/10.1016/j.evalprogplan.2016.12.009.

- ***Relevant***: Your goal should align with your values, interests, and overall life vision. If your goal doesn't resonate with you on a deeper level, you're less likely to stay motivated.
- ***Time-Bound***: A deadline for your goal not only instills a sense of urgency but also helps you maintain focus.

Why SMART Goals Work

SMART goals provide a framework for turning your dreams into actionable plans. They provide clarity, focus, and a sense of direction, which are all essential for maintaining motivation. When you have a specific, measurable, achievable, relevant, and time-bound goal, you're more likely to:

- ***Stay focused and on track***: A clear goal gives you a target to aim for and helps you prioritize your efforts.
- ***Measure progress and celebrate milestones***: Measurable goals allow you to track your progress, which can boost your motivation and reinforce positive behavior.
- ***Stay motivated***: Achievable and relevant goals are more likely to keep you engaged and excited about your journey.
- ***Avoid procrastination***: Time-bound goals create a sense of urgency and prevent you from putting things off indefinitely.

Crafting Your SMART Goals

Take some time to reflect on your aspirations and dreams. What do you truly want to achieve in life? Once you have a clear vision, start breaking it down into smaller, more manageable goals. Use the SMART criteria to ensure your goals are well-defined and actionable.

Here are some examples of SMART goals :
- "I will run a 5K race in under 30 minutes by the end of the year."
- "I will increase my monthly sales by 15% within the next six months."
- "I will learn to speak conversational Spanish by taking online classes for 30 minutes each day for the next year."

- "I will write a 50,000-word novel by the end of the next two years."
- "I will save $10,000 for a down payment on a house within the next three years."

Remember, your goals should be personal and meaningful to you. Don't be afraid to dream big, but make sure your goals are grounded in reality and align with your values and aspirations.

By setting SMART goals, you're not just creating a to-do list; you're charting a course for your life. You're taking control of your destiny and empowering yourself to create the future you desire. So, grab a pen and start brainstorming. Get ready to turn your dreams into reality!

Under this text, you will find the canvas for your goals. Use it to chart your course and illuminate the dreams and aspirations that set your soul ablaze.

I will: _____

_____

_____

_____

_____

_____

_____

_____

_____

_____

Objectives: Your Roadmap to Success

Objectives act as steppingstones, guiding you towards your ultimate vision and providing a sense of progress and accomplishment along the way. By dissecting your overarching goals into smaller, more specific objectives, you make them less daunting and more achievable.

But don't let the task at hand be overwhelming. The daunting task of eating an elephant seems impossible at first glance. The sheer size and enormity of the task can paralyze us with fear and doubt. Desmond Tutu is credited with popularizing the adage, "The only way to eat an elephant is one bite at a time." This simple yet profound statement reminds us that even the most overwhelming challenges can be overcome by breaking them down into smaller, more manageable steps.

By focusing on taking that first bite—that initial action—we set in motion a chain reaction of progress that gradually leads us to our ultimate goal. Remember, every journey begins with a single step, and every elephant is devoured one bite at a time.

Develop a detailed plan outlining the steps you need to take to reach each goal. This roadmap should include objectives, deadlines, milestones, and potential obstacles you might encounter. This approach allows you to tackle your goals one bite at a time.

Harnessing Visual Tools for Effective Goal Setting
Mind Maps

Mind maps are an excellent tool for setting goals because they provide a visual and structured approach to organizing and planning. Here's how it can be helpful:

- ***Captures ideas and connections***: A mind map starts with a central idea (your main goal) and branches out to capture related ideas, sub-goals, and actions. This helps you explore different aspects of your goal and see how they are interconnected.

- ***Organizes thoughts and priorities***: Mind maps can help you organize your thoughts, prioritize tasks, and identify the most important steps you need to take to achieve your goal.
- ***Stimulates creativity***: The visual nature of a mind map can stimulate creativity and help you generate new ideas and approaches to your goals.

Turning Your Dreams into Reality

The journey from dream to goal is not always easy, but it is undoubtedly rewarding. By setting clear goals, taking consistent action, and maintaining unwavering focus, we can turn our dreams into reality and create a life that is both meaningful and fulfilling. The path may be long and winding, but with each step we take, we move closer to our desired destination, one goal at a time.

Embracing the ACTDRIVE principles—acting with purpose and drive—allows us to navigate this journey with resilience and determination. Remember, it's not about sprinting towards the finish line but rather about enjoying the process of growth and transformation that unfolds along the way.

Here's an example of one of my dreams and my method of defining the defining the goals and setting specific objectives:

- **Dream**: Become a published author
  - **Goal**: Write and publish a novel
    - **Objectives**:
      - Outline the plot and characters by the end of the month
      - Write 500 words per day
      - Complete the first draft in six months
      - Decide to self-publish or finding publisher
      - Find an editor and illustrator

By breaking down the larger goal (i.e., writing and publishing a book) into smaller objectives, you create a clear roadmap for your journey. This makes the goal seem less daunting and more achievable. Do you remember how to eat an elephant? This approach allows you to measure your progress and adjust your approach as needed.

If your goal is to lose weight, define weekly exercise routines and meal plans. If it's a dream vacation, outline the destinations, activities, and budget. By breaking down your dream into smaller, manageable pieces, you'll transform an overwhelming aspiration into a series of achievable tasks. This approach provides a sense of direction and progress, making the journey towards your ultimate goal less daunting and more rewarding.

Please share an example of one of your dreams, and how you've broken it down into specific goals and objectives. This will help us explore your aspirations in more detail and connect them to your deeper values and motivations.

Use this white space to list your objectives:

_____

_____

_____

_____

_____

_____

_____

_____

_____

By breaking down your dream into smaller, manageable pieces, you'll transform an overwhelming aspiration into a series of achievable tasks. This approach provides a sense of direction and progress, making the journey towards your ultimate goal less daunting and more rewarding.

But setting goals is just the beginning. To truly turn our dreams into reality, we must take consistent and deliberate action. This means taking some type of meaningful action towards those goals every day.

Remember, success requires discipline, perseverance, and a willingness to embrace challenges and setbacks as opportunities for growth. We must be willing to step outside of our comfort zones. This means learning new skills and adapting to changing circumstances.

Sarah's Bookstore Dream: Taking the First Step

Sarah had always dreamed of owning a charming bookstore in her small town—a cozy haven where book lovers could gather, read, and sip coffee. She envisioned shelves filled with a curated selection of books, comfortable reading nooks, and the aroma of freshly brewed coffee wafting through the air. It was a beautiful dream, but for years, it remained just that—a dream.

Life kept getting in the way. Sarah was busy with her full-time job, family responsibilities, and the everyday demands that left her little time or energy to pursue her passion. The dream of the bookstore stayed tucked away in the back of her mind, a distant fantasy overshadowed by the practicalities of life.

One evening, while leafing through an old journal, Sarah rediscovered a forgotten entry where she had vividly described her dream of opening a bookstore. The memories and emotions flooded back, as vibrant as if she had written them yesterday. She realized with a start that, despite the years that had passed, her passion for the bookstore remained as strong as ever. It was a moment of clarity, a realization that she had allowed fear and procrastination to steal years of potential joy.

Determined to take the first step, Sarah decided to share her dream with her best friend, Lisa. Over coffee, she poured out her heart, detailing her vision and her fears.

"Lisa, I've been thinking a lot lately about that dream I had of opening a bookstore. You remember, right?" Sarah sighed deeply.

Lisa smiled, "Of course, I do! You've talked about it for years. Why do you bring it up now?"

Sarah nervously fiddled with her coffee cup. "I found my old journal the other day and read through the pages where I wrote all about it. The vision, the excitement—it's still there, deep inside me. But I feel like I've let fear and life get in the way."

Lisa reached out to touch Sarah's hand. "Sarah, that's a beautiful dream. What's holding you back?"

Sarah looked down, "I guess it's the usual—fear of failing, not knowing where to start, and being too busy with work and family."

Lisa nodded, "I get that. But have you thought about starting small? You don't have to open a bookstore overnight."

Sarah looked curious, "What do you mean?"

Lisa continued enthusiastically, "Well, what about starting with something manageable? Like an online bookstore or a blog, you review books and build a community of book lovers. You can gradually work towards your bigger dream."

Sarah was thoughtful, "That sounds more doable. But I'm not sure where to begin."

Lisa grinned, "How about this: Spend your weekends visiting local bookstores, talking to the owners, and learning from their experiences. You can also start attending community events and book fairs. It'll give you a feel for the business and help you network."

Sarah smiled, "That's a great idea! I could even start curating a selection of books and selling them online. It'll be a way to test the waters."

"Exactly!" Lisa exclaimed. "Plus, you can use social media to share your journey, connect with other book lovers, and build your brand. Sarah, baby steps! Every little step counts."

Sarah felt more confident. "You're right, Lisa. I've been letting fear stop me for too long. I'm going to start this weekend by visiting that new bookstore downtown and talking to the owner."

Lisa raised her coffee cup, "That's the spirit! And remember, I'm here to support you every step of the way. We can even brainstorm together if you need ideas or just someone to listen to."

Sarah clinked her cup with Lisa's, "Thanks, Lisa. Your support means the world to me. I feel like I can finally start making my dream a reality."

"To new beginnings and the journey toward your bookstore dream!" Lisa toasted.

"To new beginnings!" Sarah echoed with a smile.

Sarah started by dedicating her weekends to visiting local bookstores and talking to the owners. She asked questions, learned about the challenges and rewards, and gathered valuable insights. She also began attending community events and book fairs to understand her potential customers' preferences.

Slowly but surely, Sarah's confidence grew. She set up a small online bookstore, curating a selection of books that reflected her taste and the interests of her community. She started a blog to share her love for books, offering reviews and recommendations. Her weekends were now filled with activities that brought her joy and inched her closer to her dream.

Within a year, Sarah's online bookstore gained a loyal following. Encouraged by the positive response, she hosted pop-up bookstore events in local cafes, testing the waters and building her brand. Each event was a learning experience, helping her refine her vision and connect with her community.

Finally, after two years of hard work, saving, and planning, Sarah found the perfect location for her bookstore. It was a quaint little shop on the main street, just as she had imagined. With the support of her family, friends, and the community she had built, Sarah opened the doors to her dream bookstore.

The journey was far from easy, and there were many challenges along the way. But Sarah's story is a testament to the power of taking that first step, no matter how small. It's about the importance of turning dreams into actionable goals and persevering through the obstacles.

Sarah's journey toward achieving her dream of owning a bookstore started with a single step: reigniting her passion and seeking support. Her story highlights the importance of defining your dreams, taking incremental steps, and building momentum over time.

As you embark on your 17-day journey, remember that every dream begins with a single step. What is the first small action you can take toward your dream this week? Write it down, share it with someone you trust, and start moving toward your goal. Like Sarah, you have the power to transform your dreams into reality.

Conclusion

Today, we've taken a significant step in our journey from dream to destination. We've learned the importance of setting SMART goals, breaking them down into manageable objectives, and using visual tools like mind maps to chart our course. We've also seen how Sarah's story exemplifies the power of taking that first step, no matter how small, towards our dreams.

As you continue on your 17-day journey, remember that turning your dreams into reality is a process that requires clarity, focus, and consistent action. By setting SMART goals, creating a roadmap, and taking those first small steps, you'll gain momentum and confidence, propelling yourself towards your desired destination.

Tomorrow, we'll delve into the science behind self-motivation, exploring the neurochemicals that fuel our drive, the psychological factors that influence our behavior, and the environmental influences that shape our motivation levels. Get ready to unlock the secrets of your inner drive and discover the power of self-motivation.

PART II:
R - REIMAGINE YOUR POSSIBILITIES

"The only person you are destined to become
is the person you decide to be."

—Ralph Waldo Emerson

DAY 3:
THE SCIENCE BEHIND SELF-MOTIVATION

What is self-motivation?

In the previous chapter, we embarked on an exciting journey to turn dreams into actionable goals, exploring the ACTDRIVE method and the art of setting SMART goals. By now, you should have a clearer vision of your desired future and the tools to start turning your dreams into reality. If you haven't quite identified your desired future yet, that's okay. For some, this process requires a deeper exploration of their dreams and aspirations. If you find yourself in this situation, don't hesitate to revisit Day 1 and complete the exercises again. Take your time, be patient with yourself, and allow your dreams to unfold organically. Remember, this journey is about self-discovery and growth, and there's no right or wrong timeline.

Today, we'll dive into the fascinating world of self-motivation—the internal drive that pushes us to take action and persevere, echoing Sam Levenson's wise words: "Don't watch the clock; do what it does. Keep going." This drive isn't reliant on external rewards or recognition; it stems from a deep-seated desire to grow, learn, and achieve your full potential, moving forward with unwavering determination, just as the clock tirelessly ticks on.

The Anatomy of Self-Motivation

Self-motivation isn't a singular entity; it's a complex interplay of various factors[5]. Let's delve into the key components that contribute to this powerful force:

- *Intrinsic Motivation*: This is the most potent form of motivation, stemming from your genuine interest and passion for the task at hand. When you're intrinsically motivated, you engage in activities because you find them inherently enjoyable and fulfilling, not for external rewards or pressures[6]. As Steve Jobs famously said, "The only way to do great work is to love what you do. If you haven't found it yet, keep looking. Don't settle."
- *Positive Self-Talk*: The way you talk to yourself plays a crucial role in your motivation levels. Replacing negative self-talk with positive affirmations can significantly boost your self-confidence and drive. As Louise Hay wisely said, "You have been criticizing yourself for years, and it hasn't worked. Try approving of yourself and see what happens."
- *Resilience*: The ability to bounce back from setbacks is a hallmark of self-motivated individuals. Viewing failures as learning opportunities rather than roadblocks fosters resilience and a determination to succeed. As Steve Maraboli aptly put it, "Life doesn't get easier or more forgiving, we get stronger and more resilient."
- *Discipline*: While motivation is essential for sparking action, discipline is what sustains progress when motivation inevitably fades. Developing the discipline to stick to your routines and habits, even when faced with challenges or a lack of enthusiasm, is key to long-term success. As Jim Rohn eloquently stated, "Discipline is the bridge between goals and accomplishment."

---

5   Robert Grassinger et al., "Interplay of Intrinsic Motivation and Well-Being at School," *Motivation and Emotion* 48, no. 2 (2024), https://doi.org/10.1007/s11031-024-10057-2.
6   Betsy Ng, "The Neuroscience of Growth Mindset and Intrinsic Motivation," *Brain Sciences* 8, no. 2 (2018), https://doi.org/10.3390/brainsci8020020.

- ***Practice Self-Care***: Taking care of your physical and mental well-being is crucial for maintaining high levels of motivation and overall productivity. Prioritize getting enough sleep, regular exercise, a balanced diet, and stress-management techniques. As Katie Reed wisely said, "Self-care is giving the world the best of you, instead of what's left of you."

The Neurochemical Symphony of Motivation

Ever wondered why some days you feel like you could conquer the world, while other days getting out of bed seems like a monumental task? It turns out there's a fascinating scientific explanation for these fluctuations in motivation. In this next section, we'll delve into the intricate workings of the brain. We'll explore the neurotransmitters and hormones that fuel our drive, as well as the psychological and environmental factors that influence our motivation levels.

At the heart of self-motivation lies a complex interplay of neurochemicals[7]. One of the key players is dopamine, often referred to as the "motivation molecule." When we anticipate or experience something rewarding, our brains release dopamine, creating a sense of pleasure and reinforcement that drives us to repeat the behavior. This dopamine rush is what fuels our pursuit of goals, from acing a test to landing a promotion to simply checking off items on our to-do list.

But dopamine isn't the only neurochemical involved in motivation. Serotonin, known for its role in mood regulation, also plays a part. When our serotonin levels are balanced, we tend to feel happier, more optimistic, and more motivated to take on challenges. Additionally, endorphins, the body's natural painkillers, can trigger feelings of euphoria and accomplishment, further boosting our drive to succeed.

---

[7] J. David Pincus, "The Structure of Human Motivation," *BMC Psychology* 11, no. 1 (2023), https://doi.org/10.1186/s40359-023-01346-5.

The Psychology of Motivation

While neurochemicals lay the foundation for motivation, our thoughts and beliefs also play a crucial role. Our self-efficacy, or belief in our ability to succeed, significantly impacts our motivation levels[8]. When we believe we can achieve a goal, we're more likely to put in the effort required to reach it. Conversely, if we doubt our abilities, we may hesitate to even try.

Our values, interests, and passions also contribute to our motivation. When we engage in activities that align with our core values, we experience a sense of purpose and meaning that fuels our drive[9]. Similarly, pursuing our interests and passions can spark intrinsic motivation—the desire to do something for the sheer joy of it rather than for external rewards or recognition.

Environmental Influences

By understanding the science behind self-motivation, we can gain greater control over our drive and harness it to achieve our goals. We can learn to identify the neurochemical triggers that motivate us, cultivate a positive mindset, surround ourselves with supportive influences, and create an environment that fosters productivity and creativity.

Our environment plays a crucial role in shaping our motivation. A supportive environment, filled with positive influences, encouragement, and like-minded individuals, can significantly boost our self-efficacy and propel us towards our goals[10]. Conversely, a negative environment, marked by crit-

---

8   Sara Madeleine Kristensen et al., "Academic Stress, Academic Self-Efficacy, and Psychological Distress: A Moderated Mediation of Within-Person Effects," *Journal of Youth and Adolescence* 52, no. 7 (2023), https://doi.org/10.1007/s10964-023-01770-1.

9   Detlef Urhahne and Lisette Wijnia, "Theories of Motivation in Education: An Integrative Framework," *Educational Psychology Review* 35, no. 2 (2023), https://doi.org/10.1007/s10648-023-09767-9.

10 Heqiao Wang and Gary A. Troia, "How Students' Writing Motivation, Teachers' Personal and Professional Attributes, and Writing Instruction Impact Student Writing Achievement: A Two-Level Hierarchical Linear Modeling Study," *Frontiers in Psychology* 14 (2023), https://doi.org/10.3389/fpsyg.2023.1213929.

icism, negativity, or discouragement, can stifle our enthusiasm and undermine our drive.

As Jim Rohn famously stated, "You are the average of the five people you spend the most time with," highlighting the importance of choosing our company wisely. Surrounding ourselves with supportive friends, mentors, and colleagues who believe in our abilities and encourage our growth can make all the difference in achieving success.

The Peak of John's Ambition: A Mount Rainier Ascent

John had always felt the allure of the mountains; their towering presence was a silent invitation to conquer them. The summit of Mount Rainier, a glistening jewel in the Washington landscape, held a particular fascination for him. Yet, with a demanding job and life's responsibilities, it remained a distant dream.

Catching up with Emily, an experienced mountaineer and old friend, over coffee one day, John couldn't contain his yearning any longer. "Emily," he sighed, "I've always dreamt of standing atop Rainier, but it seems impossible with my schedule and lack of training."

Emily smiled knowingly, "John, every climber starts somewhere. It's a journey of small steps, building skills and confidence. Have you been climbing lately?"

"Only some indoor bouldering," John admitted. "Rainier seems a world away from that."

"It is," Emily agreed, "but every climb, no matter how small, brings you closer. How about starting with some local outdoor climbs? I'm happy to guide you."

Invigorated by Emily's encouragement, John took the first step. Weekends were now filled with excursions to nearby crags, tackling progressively challenging routes under Emily's watchful eye. With each climb, John's skills sharpened, and his confidence soared.

"I'm really enjoying this," John confessed to Emily one afternoon, as they basked in the afterglow of a successful ascent. "It's hard, but so rewarding."

"That's the spirit," Emily beamed. "Let's map out a long-term training plan to keep you on track for Rainier."

And so, John embarked on a structured training regimen, incorporating strength training, cardio, and regular climbing sessions. His mornings started with workouts, and weekends were dedicated to outdoor adventures. He noticed a significant improvement in his strength and stamina.

"I'm feeling stronger and more focused," he reported to Emily, a newfound determination in his voice. "Rainier doesn't seem so out of reach anymore."

Of course, the journey wasn't without its setbacks. Unfavorable weather conditions occasionally thwarted their plans, and some routes proved more challenging than anticipated. But John viewed these as valuable lessons, not failures. "Every challenge is an opportunity to learn and grow," he mused, a testament to his resilience.

As the months passed, John's progress was undeniable. He relished the sense of accomplishment that came with each conquered peak, his confidence steadily rising with every ascent.

"I tackled some of the tougher local climbs," he proudly told Emily. "Rainier is getting closer every day."

"You've come so far, John," Emily praised. "Your passion and dedication are truly inspiring. Keep going!"

John's journey was a powerful reminder of the importance of starting small and pursuing dreams one step at a time. Through self-motivation, unwavering support, and a willingness to embrace challenges, he transformed a seemingly unattainable goal into a tangible reality. Climbing had become more than just a hobby; it was a source of joy, a testament to his perseverance, and a symbol of what he could achieve when he set his mind to it.

As John stood at the base of Mount Rainier, ready to embark on the ultimate challenge, he couldn't help but feel a surge of gratitude for the journey that had brought him to this point. "Thank you, Emily," he whispered, a silent acknowledgment of the pivotal role she had played. "Rainier awaits."

With a deep breath, John began his ascent, his heart filled with anticipation and his spirit brimming with the knowledge that he was ready to reach the peak of his ambition.

Reaching the summit and gazing out at the breathtaking panorama below, John felt an overwhelming sense of accomplishment and profound humility. The arduous climb had not only tested his physical limits but had also revealed the depths of his own resilience and determination. He realized that the journey itself, with its trials and triumphs, had been just as valuable as the destination. As he descended, John knew that this experience would forever shape his life, fueling his passion for adventure and reminding him that with dedication and perseverance, even the loftiest dreams can be realized.

As you embark on your 17-day journey, remember that every dream begins with a single step. Identify your motivations, set realistic goals, and seek support from those around you. Embrace the challenges, celebrate your progress, and find joy in the process. Like John, you have the power to transform your dreams into reality.

Conclusion

Today, we delved into the fascinating science behind self-motivation, exploring the intricate interplay of neurochemicals, psychological factors, and environmental influences that shape our drive. We learned that motivation isn't just a fleeting feeling but a complex system that can be understood and harnessed to achieve our goals. By recognizing the role of dopamine, serotonin, and endorphins, we can identify the activities and experiences that naturally boost our motivation. By cultivating a positive mindset, setting meaningful goals, and surrounding ourselves with supportive influences, we can create an environment that fosters lasting motivation and propels us towards success.

As you continue your journey, remember that self-motivation is not a fixed trait but a dynamic force that can be cultivated and strengthened over time. By applying the insights and strategies we've explored today, you can unlock your inner drive, overcome obstacles, and achieve your full potential.

Tomorrow, we'll delve deeper into the different types of motivation, exploring the distinction between intrinsic and extrinsic motivation and how they can work together to fuel your drive. Get ready to discover the power of aligning your actions with your passions and values, as well as how to create a sustainable and fulfilling path toward your goals.

Notes

"The only way to do great work
is to love what you do."

—Steve Jobs

DAY 4:
FUELING YOUR FIRE: INTRINSIC VS. EXTRINSIC MOTIVATION

In the previous chapter, we delved into the fascinating science behind self-motivation, exploring the intricate interplay of neurochemicals, psychological factors, and environmental influences that shape our drive. We learned that motivation isn't just a fleeting feeling but a complex system that can be understood and harnessed to achieve our goals.

Today, we'll take a closer look at two key types of motivation: intrinsic and extrinsic. Have you ever pursued a goal simply because it brought you joy or satisfaction, without any external rewards or pressures? Or perhaps you've been driven by the promise of recognition, financial gain, or avoiding negative consequences? These two scenarios highlight the fundamental difference between intrinsic and extrinsic motivation, two powerful forces that shape our behavior and drive us towards our objectives. You can create a sustainable and fulfilling path to your goals by understanding and leveraging both.

Intrinsic Motivation: The Joy of the Journey

Intrinsic motivation comes from within. It's the innate desire to engage in an activity because it's inherently enjoyable, interesting, or personally meaningful. When we're intrinsically motivated, we act for the sake of the activity itself, not for any external rewards or incentives[11]. We derive pleasure,

---

[11] Isabel Mercader-Rubio et al., "Intrinsic Motivation: Knowledge, Achievement, and Experimentation in Sports Science Students—relations with Emotional Intelligence," *Behavioral Sciences* 13, no. 7 (2023), https://doi.org/10.3390/bs13070589.

satisfaction, and a sense of accomplishment from the process of learning, growing, and mastering new skills.

Examples of intrinsic motivation include :
- Immersing yourself in a round of golf, relishing the challenge and the connection with nature.
- Finding tranquility while sitting on the beach, mesmerized by the beauty of a sunset.
- Getting lost in the pages of a book is purely for the joy of the story and the escape it provides.
- Engaging in a sport is not for competition, but for the game's love and social connection.
- Pursuing creative outlets like painting or music is fueled by the desire to express yourself and explore your imagination.
- Embracing the challenge of learning a new language is driven by a fascination with different cultures and a thirst for knowledge.
- Volunteering your time and energy for a cause you believe in means finding fulfillment in making a positive impact on the world.

These activities are intrinsically motivating because they are driven by internal rewards like joy, satisfaction, personal growth, and a sense of purpose rather than external incentives like money or recognition[12].

Extrinsic Motivation: The Lure of Rewards

Extrinsic motivation, on the other hand, comes from external factors. It's the drive to engage in an activity to earn a reward or avoid punishment. These rewards can be tangible, such as money, prizes, or recognition, or intangible, such as praise, approval, or status. Extrinsic motivation can be a powerful motivator, especially when the rewards are significant or the consequences of failure are severe.

---

12 Mercader-Rubio et al., "Intrinsic Motivation."

Examples of extrinsic motivation include:
- Studying hard to get good grades and earn a scholarship.
- Working overtime to get a bonus or promotion.
- Exercising to lose weight and improve your appearance.
- Competing in a race to win a medal or trophy.
- Following rules and regulations to avoid getting into trouble.

The Synergy of Intrinsic and Extrinsic Motivation

In many situations, intrinsic and extrinsic motivation can work in harmony, amplifying each other's effects. For instance, a writer may be intrinsically motivated by the joy of storytelling and self-expression, but the prospect of publishing a book (extrinsic reward) can further fuel their determination. Similarly, a student might be intrinsically curious about a subject, while the promise of good grades (extrinsic motivator) encourages them to study harder.

The Potential Pitfalls of Over-Reliance on Extrinsic Motivation

However, relying too heavily on extrinsic rewards can backfire. When external incentives become the primary focus, they can overshadow the inherent joy and satisfaction that come from the activity itself. This can lead to a decrease in intrinsic motivation and a reliance on external validation for continued effort[13].

For example, a child who initially loved playing the piano for the sheer enjoyment of it might lose interest if they are constantly pressured to practice for recitals and competitions. The focus shifts from the joy of music to the pursuit of external recognition, potentially diminishing the intrinsic motivation that once fueled their passion.

---

13 Yuxia Liu et al., "Do Immediate External Rewards Really Enhance Intrinsic Motivation?," *Frontiers in Psychology* 13 (2022), https://doi.org/10.3389/fpsyg.2022.853879.

Striking a Balance

The key is to strike a balance between intrinsic and extrinsic motivation. Recognize and celebrate the internal rewards that come from pursuing activities you genuinely enjoy, while also acknowledging the role that external incentives can play in providing additional drive and focus[14].

To foster intrinsic motivation, create an environment that supports autonomy, competence, and relatedness. This means allowing yourself the freedom to pursue activities you find interesting, setting challenging yet achievable goals, and connecting with others who share your passions.

By understanding and leveraging both intrinsic and extrinsic motivation, you can create a sustainable and fulfilling path towards your goals. Remember, the most rewarding journey is often the one that is driven by a combination of internal passion and external encouragement.

Finding Your Inner Drive

Take some time to reflect on your own motivations. What activities do you find genuinely enjoyable? What are your passions and values? By identifying your inner drive, you can set meaningful goals that resonate with you on a deeper level. Use the white space after each question to write down and acknowledge your motivations.

Past Experiences:

1. Recall a time when you felt truly passionate and energized about a project or activity. What made it so fulfilling?

___

___

___

---

14 Mercader-Rubio et al., "Intrinsic Motivation."

2. Describe a situation where you felt demotivated or disengaged. What factors contributed to this feeling?

_____

_____

_____

3. What are some of your proudest accomplishments, and what motivated you to achieve them?

_____

_____

_____

Personal Values:

1. What are the top three values that guide your life?

_____

_____

_____

2. How do your current goals and activities align with these values?

_____

_____

_____

3. Are there any areas where your actions are not consistent with your values?

_____

_____

_____

Ideal Future:

1. What does your ideal day look like?

_____

_____

_____

2. What kind of work or activities would bring you the most joy and fulfillment?

_____

_____

_____

3. Where do you see yourself in five years, and what steps can you take to get there?

_____

_____

_____

Obstacles and Challenges:

1. What are the main obstacles or challenges that you face in pursuing your goals?

_____

_____

_____

2. How can you overcome these obstacles?

_____

_____

_____

3. What support systems or resources could you leverage to help you stay motivated?

_____

_____

_____

Personal Growth:

1. What skills or knowledge would you like to develop further?

_____

_____

_____

2. How can you incorporate these interests into your current goals or activities?

_____

_____

_____

3. What steps can you take to create a more supportive and motivating environment for yourself?

_____

_____

_____

Reflecting on these questions will make the pursuit of your goals more fulfilling, but it will also increase your chances of success. Remember, the most sustainable and rewarding path is often the one that is fueled by intrinsic motivation.

Use the white space to write down any additional thoughts:

_____

_____

_____

_____

_____

Now that you've taken the time to reflect on your motivations, it's time to put that self-awareness into action. Use your newfound understanding of your intrinsic drivers to set goals that truly resonate with you. Embrace activities that bring you joy, utilize your unique skills and talents, and pursue causes that ignite your passion. By aligning your actions with your inner drive, you'll not only experience greater fulfillment in your pursuits, but you'll also unlock your full potential for success. Remember, your motivation is your most valuable asset; nurture it, embrace it, and let it guide you towards a life that is both meaningful and rewarding.

Liam's Music Passion: Finding Joy Beyond Rewards

Liam had always been musically inclined. Ever since he was a child, he loved the sound of instruments, the rhythm of melodies, and the way music could evoke emotions. He played the guitar and piano, often performing at local events and gatherings. However, as he grew older, his love for music started to feel more like a chore. The pressure to perform flawlessly and the constant chase for recognition began to overshadow his initial joy.

One evening, after a particularly stressful day at work, Liam sat down with his guitar. He strummed a few chords, feeling the weight of expectations bear down on him. Just then, his old friend, Emily, called.

"Hey, Liam! How's it going?" Emily asked. "Haven't heard you play in a while."

Liam sighed, "Honestly, Emily, I've been struggling. Music used to be my escape, but now it feels like a burden. It's all about impressing people and getting applause."

"I get it," Emily replied empathetically. "It's tough when something you love becomes stressful. But remember why you started in the first place. Why did you pick up the guitar?"

Liam paused, reflecting on his past. "I picked it up because it made me happy. I loved the sound, the feeling of creating something beautiful."

"Exactly!" Emily exclaimed. "You didn't start playing for the applause or the recognition. You played it because you loved it. Maybe you need to reconnect with that joy."

Rediscovering the Joy

Emily's words resonated with Liam. He realized he needed to shift his focus from external rewards to the intrinsic joy of playing music. The next day, he decided to visit a local park, taking only his guitar with him. No audience, no expectations—just him and his music.

As he sat under a tree, he started playing. The melodies flowed effortlessly, and for the first time in a long while, he felt the pure joy of playing. It wasn't about being perfect; it was about expressing himself and feeling the music.

"This feels right," Liam thought to himself. "This is why I started playing in the first place."

Over the next few weeks, Liam made it a habit to play in the park. He experimented with new tunes, wrote his own songs, and even played just for the birds and the breeze. He found that without the pressure to perform, his creativity flourished.

A New Perspective

One day, Emily joined him at the park.

"It's great to see you enjoying music again, Liam," she said. "You look so much happier."

"Thanks, Emily," Liam replied. "Playing here, away from all the pressure, has helped me reconnect with why I love music. I'm not playing for anyone but myself."

"That's wonderful," Emily said. "Have you thought about sharing this with others? Not for the recognition, but to inspire them to find their own joy in music."

Liam's eyes lit up. "I have, actually. I've been thinking of starting a music circle. A place where people can come together to play, learn, and just enjoy music without any judgment or pressure."

Building a Community

Inspired by this idea, Liam started organizing weekly music circles at the park. He invited friends, fellow musicians, and anyone interested in music to join. The gatherings became a space for people to share their love for music, learn from each other, and play without the fear of judgment.

"Liam, this music circle is amazing," one participant shared. "I've always been afraid to play in front of others, but here, it feels different."

Another participant agreed, "Yeah, it's so refreshing to just enjoy the music and not worry about being perfect."

Liam smiled, "That's exactly why I started this. Music should be about joy and connection, not just performance. I'm glad you all feel the same way."

Through this journey, Liam rediscovered his passion for music. He learned that true fulfillment comes from intrinsic motivation—the joy of doing something for its own sake, not for external rewards or recognition. His music circle thrived, and he found immense satisfaction in sharing his love for music with others and creating a supportive community.

As you navigate your own journey, remember the importance of intrinsic motivation. Find joy in the process, embrace the love for what you do, and let go of the pressure to meet external expectations. Like Liam, you can transform your passion into a source of genuine happiness and fulfillment.

Conclusion

Today, we explored the fascinating interplay between intrinsic and extrinsic motivation, two powerful forces that shape our behavior and drive us towards our goals. We learned that intrinsic motivation, fueled by internal rewards like joy, satisfaction, and personal growth, is the most sustainable and fulfilling source of drive. While extrinsic motivation, driven by external rewards or punishments, can be effective in the short term, it's important to strike a balance and not rely solely on external validation.

As you continue your journey, reflect on your own motivations. What drives you? What brings you joy and fulfillment? By understanding your intrinsic and extrinsic motivators, you can make conscious choices that align with your values and passions, leading to a more meaningful and rewarding life.

Tomorrow, we'll delve into the concept of self-efficacy, the belief in our ability to succeed, and how it plays a crucial role in achieving our goals. Get ready to unlock the power of self-belief and discover how to cultivate unwavering confidence in your abilities.

"Whether you think you can or you think you can't, you're right."

—Henry Ford

DAY 5:
IGNITING THE ENGINE: BUILDING SELF-EFFICACY FOR LASTING MOTIVATION

In the previous chapter, we explored the fascinating world of motivation, delving into the differences between intrinsic and extrinsic motivators. We discovered that while external rewards can be enticing, true and lasting motivation often stems from within. We learned about how important it is to align our actions with our passions and values, and how this alignment can lead to a more fulfilling and purposeful life.

Today, we'll shift our focus to self-efficacy—the unwavering belief in our ability to succeed. This belief is a crucial ingredient for lasting motivation. Imagine yourself standing at the foot of a mountain, gazing up at its towering peak. The thought of reaching the summit may seem daunting, even impossible. But deep down, a flicker of belief ignites—a belief that with the right tools, training, and mindset, you can conquer this challenge.

Self-efficacy is not just about having confidence; it's about having a realistic and positive assessment of your capabilities. It's the conviction that you can overcome obstacles, learn new skills, and achieve your goals, even in the face of adversity. When you possess high self-efficacy, you're more likely to set ambitious goals, persevere through setbacks, and ultimately achieve success[15].

---

15 "The Relationship of Academic Self-Efficacy, Goal Orientation, and Personal Goal Setting Among High School Students," *Frontiers in Educational Research* 4, no. 11 (2021), https://doi.org/10.25236/fer.2021.041109.

The Four Pillars of Self-Efficacy

According to psychologist Albert Bandura[16], self-efficacy is built upon four main sources:

1. *Mastery Experiences*: The most powerful source of self-efficacy is the experience of successfully mastering a task or challenge. Each time you overcome an obstacle, you gain confidence in your abilities and strengthen your belief in yourself
2. *Vicarious Experiences*: Observing others succeed can also boost your self-efficacy. Seeing someone similar to you achieve a goal can inspire you and demonstrate that success is possible.
3. *Social Persuasion*: Encouragement and positive feedback from others can bolster your self-efficacy. When people believe in you and your abilities, it can reinforce your own self-belief and motivate you to persevere.
4. *Emotional and Physiological States*: Your emotional and physical state can influence your self-efficacy. When you're feeling stressed, anxious, or fatigued, you may doubt your abilities. Conversely, when you're feeling calm, confident, and energized, you're more likely to believe in yourself.

Building Your Self-Efficacy Muscle

Just like any other muscle, self-efficacy can be strengthened through practice and training. Here are some strategies for building your self-efficacy muscle:

- *Set realistic and achievable goals*: Build confidence and momentum by starting small and gradually increasing the difficulty of the goal.
- *Break down large tasks into smaller steps*: This will make the task seem less daunting and give you a sense of progress as you complete each step.

---

16 Anita Dyb Linge et al., "Bandura's Self-Efficacy Model Used to Explore Participants' Experiences of Health, Lifestyle, and Work After Attending a Vocational Rehabilitation Program with Lifestyle Intervention – a Focus Group Study," *Journal of Multidisciplinary Healthcare* Volume 14 (2021), https://doi.org/10.2147/jmdh.s334620.

- **Celebrate your successes**: Acknowledging and celebrating even the smallest victories can fuel motivation and build momentum towards greater achievements.
- **Learn from your failures**: Don't let setbacks discourage you. Instead, view them as learning opportunities and use them to identify areas for improvement.
- **Surround yourself with positive and supportive people**: Their encouragement and belief in you can reinforce your own self-efficacy.
- **Challenge negative self-talk**: Silence your self-doubt with positive affirmations and a focus on your unique talent.
- **Visualize success**: Imagine yourself achieving your goals, feeling the emotions of accomplishment and pride.
- **Invest in your physical and mental health**: A strong body and a clear mind are the foundations for unlocking your full potential and achieving self-efficacy.

Self-efficacy is not a fixed trait but rather a dynamic belief that can be cultivated and strengthened over time[17]. By adopting these strategies, you can build your self-efficacy muscle and unlock the power of lasting motivation. As you gain confidence in your abilities, you'll be empowered to set bolder goals, overcome challenges with resilience, and ultimately achieve your full potential.

Fanning the Flames: Finding Your Passion and Igniting Purpose

Have you ever felt a deep-seated yearning for something more? A longing to make a difference, to leave your mark on the world, or to do something that truly excites and fulfills you? If so, then you're likely on a quest to discover your passion.

---

17 Macário Neri Ferreira-Neto et al., "The Role of Self-Efficacy, Entrepreneurial Passion, and Creativity in Developing Entrepreneurial Intentions," *Frontiers in Psychology* 14 (2023), https://doi.org/10.3389/fpsyg.2023.1134618.

Passion is the intense enthusiasm and joy we experience when we engage in activities that resonate with our core values, interests, and talents. It's the fire that fuels our motivation, the compass that guides our decisions, and the driving force behind our most meaningful accomplishments[18]. When we're passionate about something, we're more likely to persevere through challenges, overcome obstacles, and achieve extraordinary results.

But how do we find our passion? For some, it's a lifelong journey of exploration and self-discovery. For others, it's a sudden spark that ignites unexpectedly. Regardless of the path, there are several strategies you can employ to uncover your passions and align your life with your purpose.

Unleashing Your Inner Explorer

1. ***Reflect on Your Childhood Dreams***: What did you love to do as a child? What activities brought you joy and excitement? Revisiting your childhood passions can provide valuable clues about your innate interests and talents. Use the white space to capture your thoughts.

_____

_____

_____

2. ***Identify Your Strengths and Talents***: What are you naturally good at? What skills come easily to you? Your passions often lie at the intersection of your strengths and interests.

_____

_____

_____

---

18 Ng, "The Neuroscience."

3. ***Explore New Activities***: Don't be afraid to step outside your comfort zone and try new things. Take a class, join a club, volunteer for a cause, or travel to a new place. You never know what might spark your curiosity and ignite your passion. What activities will you commit to doing within the next month?

_____

_____

_____

4. ***Follow Your Curiosity***: What topics or activities pique your interest? What do you find yourself reading about, researching, or discussing with others? Follow your curiosity and see where it leads you.

_____

_____

_____

5. ***Listen to Your Intuition***: Pay attention to your gut feelings and instincts. What activities make you feel alive and energized? What do you lose track of your time doing? Your intuition can be a powerful guide to discovering your passion.

_____

_____

_____

6. ***Seek Inspiration***: Read biographies of inspiring people, watch documentaries about those who have pursued their passions, and talk to people who are living their dreams. Their stories can ignite your own passion and show you what's possible. What people inspire you?

_____

_____

_____

7. ***Experiment and Play***: Allow yourself to experiment with different activities without pressure or expectation. Playfulness can lead to unexpected discoveries and uncover hidden passions. What new activities or hobbies could you explore without any pressure or expectations, just for the joy of discovery?

_____

_____

_____

8. ***Embrace Failure***: Don't be afraid to try and fail. Failure is a natural part of the learning process and can provide valuable insights into your strengths and weaknesses.

_____

_____

_____

9. Be Patient and Persistent: Finding your passion takes time and effort. Don't get discouraged if you don't find it overnight. Keep exploring, learning, and growing, and trust that your passion will reveal itself in due time. What steps can you take today to begin exploring your interests and uncovering your passions?

_____

_____

_____

The Transformative Power of Passion

When you discover your passion, it's like finding a hidden treasure within yourself. It can infuse your life with meaning, purpose, and joy. It can inspire you to overcome challenges, pursue your dreams with relentless determination, and make a positive impact on the world.

So, embrace the journey of self-discovery, fan the flames of your curiosity, and unlock the transformative power of passion. Your life awaits.

Rachel's Public Speaking Breakthrough: Building Confidence Step by Step

Rachel had always been terrified of public speaking. The mere thought of standing in front of an audience made her palms sweat and her heart race. Yet, deep down, she knew that conquering this fear was essential for her career advancement and personal growth. She envied her colleagues, who spoke effortlessly at meetings and conferences, wishing she could do the same.

One day, after a particularly nerve-wracking presentation at work, Rachel confided in her friend and mentor, Sarah, a confident and eloquent speaker.

"Sarah, I just don't know how you do it," Rachel sighed. "You make public speaking look so easy. I felt like I was going to faint up there today."

Sarah smiled sympathetically, "I wasn't always this confident, Rachel. It took practice and a lot of small steps to get here. You can do it too, but you have to be willing to start small and build up gradually."

Rachel asked nervously, "But where do I even start? The idea of speaking in front of people terrifies me."

Sarah suggested, "Start with small, manageable goals. Join a local Toastmasters club or take a public speaking class. These environments are supportive and designed to help you build your confidence step by step."

The First Step
Taking Sarah's advice, Rachel joined a local Toastmasters club. She attended her first meeting with trepidation, but the welcoming atmosphere helped ease her anxiety. During the session, members shared their experiences and gave speeches, offering constructive feedback to one another.

"Welcome, Rachel! We're glad to have you here," the Club President greeted her warmly. "Remember, everyone starts somewhere, and we're all here to support each other."

Rachel replied nervously, "Thank you. I'm really scared, but I know I need to do this."

Over the next few weeks, Rachel began participating in the club's activities. She started with small roles like timer and grammarian, gradually gaining familiarity with the format and the people. The supportive feedback and encouragement from fellow members boosted her confidence.

Taking the Stage

The day finally arrived for Rachel to give her first prepared speech. She was anxious, but her club members were encouraging. Sarah even came to support her.

"You've got this, Rachel," Sarah reassured her. "Just remember to breathe and take your time. We're all rooting for you."

Rachel took a deep breath, "Thanks, Sarah. I'll do my best."

As Rachel stood at the podium, she felt the familiar rush of nerves. But she remembered her preparation and the supportive faces in the audience. She began speaking, focusing on her message rather than her fear. To her surprise, the words flowed more easily than she expected.

"Good evening, everyone," Rachel began. "Today, I want to share a story about overcoming fear and finding confidence…".

When she finished, the room erupted in applause. Rachel felt a wave of relief and pride wash over her.

"Fantastic job, Rachel!" the Club President exclaimed. "You were clear, engaging, and relatable. Well done!"

Sarah hugged Rachel, "I knew you could do it! You were amazing up there."

Building Momentum

Buoyed by her success, Rachel continued to take on more speaking roles at Toastmasters. She volunteered for impromptu speaking sessions and even led a few meetings. Each experience added to her confidence and skills. She also started to apply her newfound confidence at work, speaking up more during meetings and presenting her ideas with greater assurance.

"Rachel, your presentation today was really impressive," a colleague remarked. "You've come a long way."

Rachel smiled, "Thanks! It's been a lot of hard work, but it's definitely paying off."

Reflecting on the Journey

Rachel's journey taught her the value of incremental progress and the importance of building self-efficacy. By starting with small, manageable goals and gradually increasing the challenge, she was able to overcome her fear of public speaking. Toastmasters' supportive environment and encouragement from friends like Sarah played a crucial role in her transformation.

"I'm so proud of you, Rachel," Sarah said. "You've really blossomed as a speaker."

Rachel replied, "Thank you, Sarah. I couldn't have done it without your encouragement and the support from everyone at Toastmasters. It's been an incredible journey."

Rachel's public speaking breakthrough demonstrates the power of building confidence step by step. She learned that setting achievable goals, seeking support, and celebrating small victories were key to her success. By focusing on her progress rather than her fears, Rachel transformed her anxiety into confidence and discovered her voice.

As you embark on your 17-day journey, remember that every goal is attainable with the right mindset and support. Identify your fears, break down your goals into manageable steps, and seek encouragement from those around you. Like Rachel, you have the power to overcome your challenges and achieve your dreams.

Conclusion

Today, we've explored the concept of self-efficacy, the unwavering belief in our ability to succeed, and how it plays a crucial role in achieving our goals. We've learned that self-efficacy is not just about having confidence; it's about having a realistic and positive assessment of our capabilities. It's the conviction that we can overcome obstacles, learn new skills, and achieve our goals, even in the face of adversity.

As you continue your journey, remember that self-efficacy is not a fixed trait but a dynamic belief that can be cultivated and strengthened over time. By applying the strategies we've discussed today, such as setting achievable goals, celebrating your successes, and learning from your failures, you can build your self-efficacy muscle and unlock the power of lasting motivation.

Tomorrow, we'll delve into the concept of flow, a state of heightened focus and enjoyment that can lead to peak performance and intrinsic motivation. Get ready to discover how to tap into this powerful state and unlock your full potential.

"The capacity to learn is a gift; the ability to learn is a skill; the willingness to learn is a choice."

—Brian Herbert

DAY 6:
TAPPING INTO PEAK PERFORMANCE AND INTRINSIC JOY

In the previous chapter, we explored the transformative power of self-efficacy—your unwavering belief in your ability to succeed. We uncovered the four pillars that build this essential trait: mastery experiences, vicarious experiences, social persuasion, and emotional and physiological states. By adopting strategies to strengthen your self-efficacy muscle, you learned to set realistic goals, celebrate successes, learn from failures, and maintain a positive mindset.

Today, we'll shift our focus to the exhilarating state of flow—a state of heightened focus and intrinsic joy where you become fully immersed in an activity, often losing track of time and experiencing a deep sense of satisfaction. It's that feeling of being "in the zone," where your skills and the challenge at hand are perfectly balanced, and you're operating at your peak potential.

To illustrate the power of flow, let me share a personal story. When I moved back to the NC Crystal Coast from Chicago, I was struck by a realization: I had never shared my childhood experiences of growing up on the beach with my youngest son. This sparked an idea to write a pirate book called "Calico Creek: A Quest for Pirate's Treasure," which would capture those cherished memories. As I delved into writing, I became completely absorbed in the process. Hours would melt away, and my wife would have to remind me of the time and other commitments. Even when I stepped away from my desk, my mind was still buzzing with ideas and stories. I'd awaken with stories un-spooling in my mind, eager to capture the vibrant threads before they faded. Writing became my sanctuary, a state of flow in which time dissolved and the joy of creation consumed me.

Today, we'll explore how to find and sustain this state of flow, unlocking a pathway to peak performance, intrinsic motivation, and ultimately, a more fulfilling and joyful life.

The Benefits of Flow

What is flow? Flow, also known as "being in the zone," is a mental state of complete absorption in an activity. It's characterized by a feeling of effortless concentration, enjoyment, and a sense of timelessness . When we're in flow, we're fully engaged in the present moment, our skills are perfectly matched to the challenge at hand, and we experience a deep sense of satisfaction and fulfillment.

Flow isn't just a fleeting feeling of pleasure. It has numerous benefits for both our personal and professional lives. Some of the key benefits of flow include[19]:

- **Enhanced Performance**: When we're in flow, we perform at our best. Our focus is laser-sharp, our creativity is unleashed, and we're able to tap into our full potential.
- **Increased Motivation**: Flow is intrinsically motivating. When we're enjoying what we're doing and feel a sense of progress, we're more likely to stick with it and push ourselves further.
- **Reduced Stress and Anxiety**: Flow can help us escape the worries and anxieties of daily life, providing a much-needed mental break.
- **Greater Happiness and Well-being**: Flow is associated with increased happiness, life satisfaction, and a sense of purpose.

---

19 Corinna Peifer et al., "A Scoping Review of Flow Research," *Frontiers in Psychology* 13 (2022), https://doi.org/10.3389/fpsyg.2022.815665.

How to Find Your Flow

While flow may seem elusive, there are several things you can do to increase your chances of experiencing it[20]:

1. ***Choose Activities You Enjoy***: Flow is most likely to occur when we're engaged in activities that we find intrinsically rewarding. Whether it's playing music, writing, dancing, or solving puzzles, choose activities that you genuinely enjoy.
2. ***Set Clear Goals***: Having a clear goal gives you something to focus on and strive for. It also provides a sense of purpose and direction, which can enhance your engagement and enjoyment.
3. ***Find the Right Challenge***: When our skills are perfectly matched to the task at hand, flow occurs. If the task is too easy, we get bored; if it's too difficult, we get frustrated. Find activities that challenge you but don't overwhelm you.
4. ***Eliminate Distractions***: To enter flow, you need to be fully immersed in the present moment. This means eliminating distractions like your phone, email, or social media. Create a quiet, distraction-free environment where you can focus on your task.
5. ***Focus on the Process***: Instead of focusing on the outcome, focus on the process of the activity itself. Pay attention to the sensations, thoughts, and feelings that arise as you engage in the task.
6. ***Lose Yourself in the Moment***: Let go of self-consciousness and worry about the future. Immerse yourself fully in the present moment and allow yourself to be carried away by the experience.
7. ***Practice Mindfulness***: Mindfulness meditation can help you develop the focus and attentional skills necessary for entering flow. By learning to quiet your mind and focus on the present moment, you can create the ideal conditions for flow to occur.

---

20 Larissa Bartlett et al., "Mindfulness Is Associated with Lower Stress and Higher Work Engagement in a Large Sample of Mooc Participants," *Frontiers in Psychology* 12 (2021), https://doi.org/10.3389/fpsyg.2021.724126.

Finding your flow is a journey of self-discovery. It's about identifying the activities that ignite your passion, challenging yourself to grow, and immersing yourself fully in the present moment. By cultivating the conditions for flow, you can unlock your full potential, achieve peak performance, and experience the deep satisfaction that comes from living a life of purpose and joy.

Savoring Success: Celebrating Milestones and Cultivating Gratitude

As you embark on your journey of self-motivation, it's crucial to recognize and celebrate your progress. Acknowledging your achievements, both big and small, can fuel your motivation, boost your confidence, and reinforce positive behaviors. It's also essential to cultivate an attitude of gratitude, appreciating the journey and all the lessons learned along the way.

The Power of Celebration

Celebration is more than just a feel-good activity; it's a powerful tool for reinforcing positive behavior and maintaining motivation. When we celebrate our achievements, our brains release dopamine, the "feel-good" neurotransmitter, which strengthens the neural pathways associated with the behavior, making it more likely to be repeated.

Celebrating doesn't have to be extravagant or expensive. It can be as simple as taking a moment to acknowledge your accomplishment, sharing your success with a friend or loved one, or rewarding yourself with a small treat. The key is to find ways to celebrate in a way that resonates with you and reinforces your progress.

Here are some ideas for celebrating your milestones:
- *Treat Yourself*: Indulge in a small luxury, like a massage, a special meal, or a new book.
- *Share Your Success*: Tell a friend, family member, or mentor about your achievement.

- **_Reflect on Your Journey_**: Take a moment to appreciate your progress and glean valuable insights from your experiences along the way.
- **_Reward Yourself with an Experience_**: Do something fun and exciting, like taking a weekend trip, going to a concert, or trying a new activity.
- **_Set a New Goal_**: Use your success as motivation to set a new, more challenging goal.

Cultivating Gratitude

Gratitude is the practice of recognizing and appreciating the good things in our lives. It's a powerful emotion that can improve our mental and physical health, strengthen our relationships, and enhance our overall well-being. Gratitude can also boost our motivation by shifting our focus from what we lack to what we have, fostering a sense of contentment and optimism.

Here are some ways to cultivate gratitude:

- **_Keep a Gratitude Journal_**: Write down three things you're grateful for each day.
- **_Expressing Gratitude to Others_**: Throughout my life, I've discovered two powerful truths: 1) most people are genuinely happy to help when asked, and 2) everyone loves to hear their own name. Take time to thank the people in your life who support and inspire you. A simple "thank you" can go a long way in strengthening relationships and boosting your own happiness.

Reflection:

1. Who are the people in your life who have made a positive impact?

_____

_____

_____

2. What specific actions or words of theirs are you grateful for?

_____

_____

_____

_____

3. Is there anyone you should call or send a thank-you card to today?

_____

_____

_____

_____

Mindfulness Challenge:

For the next week, commit to incorporating mindfulness into your daily routine. Here's how:

Choose a daily activity: Select one everyday activity to practice mindfulness during, such as eating a meal, walking, or brushing your teeth.

- ***Engage your senses***: Pay attention to the sights, sounds, smells, tastes, and textures of the experience. Notice the details that you might normally overlook.
- ***Be fully present***: Focus your attention on the present moment, letting go of thoughts about the past or future.
- ***Non-judgmental awareness***: Observe your thoughts and feelings without judgment. Simply observe them as they emerge and pass.

- ***Gratitude***: Express gratitude for the simple pleasures of life, such as a warm cup of coffee, a beautiful sunset, or a hug from a loved one.

Reflection:

1. What was your chosen daily activity for practicing mindfulness?

_____

_____

_____

_____

2. What did you notice about the experience when you paid full attention to it?

_____

_____

_____

_____

3. How did practicing mindfulness affect your mood and overall well-being?

_____

_____

_____

_____

4. What challenges did you encounter while practicing mindfulness, and how did you overcome them?

___

5. How can you continue to incorporate mindfulness into your daily life?

___

By celebrating your successes and cultivating gratitude, you'll create a positive feedback loop that fuels your motivation and propels you toward your goals. Remember, the journey is just as important as the destination, so take time to savor each step along the way and appreciate all that you have.

In the next chapter, we'll explore how to apply the principles of self-motivation to different areas of your life, from work and relationships to personal growth and well-being.

Notes

Chris's Artistic Flow: Finding Joy in the Creative Process

Chris was an artist at heart. From a young age, he found solace and joy in drawing and painting, losing himself in the world of colors and shapes. However, as he pursued a career in art, the pressure to meet deadlines, sell his work, and gain recognition began to overshadow his passion. He felt stuck, his creativity waning under the weight of expectations. One day, after another frustrating day in the studio, he called his friend, Jenna, a fellow artist who seemed to effortlessly balance creativity and professional success.

"Jenna, I'm struggling," Chris confessed, his voice heavy with frustration. "I used to love painting, but now it feels like a chore. The joy is gone, and I don't know how to get it back."

Jenna listened empathetically, "I understand, Chris. When art becomes work, it can lose its magic. But it doesn't have to be that way. Have you tried reconnecting with what made you love art in the first place?"

Chris sighed, "I'm not sure how. Every time I sit down to paint, all I can think about is whether it will sell or if it's good enough."

Jenna offered a gentle suggestion, "You need to find your flow again, Chris, where the process itself is the reward. Forget about the end product for a while and just enjoy creating."

Reconnecting with the Process

Taking Jenna's advice to heart, Chris decided to dedicate time each day to painting purely for himself, with no pressure to create something marketable. He cleared a corner of his studio, transforming it into a haven for personal expression. He filled it with sketchbooks, canvases, and his favorite art supplies.

"Okay, this is just for me," Chris reminded himself. "No pressure, no expectations. Just enjoy the process."

He began with simple sketches, allowing his mind to wander and his hand to move freely. As he sketched, he felt a familiar sense of calm wash over him. For the first time in months, he wasn't worried about the outcome; he was simply enjoying the act of creation.

Finding Flow

Over the next few weeks, Chris immersed himself in his personal art sessions. He experimented with different techniques and mediums, rediscovering the joy of learning and exploring new ideas. The pressure to produce something perfect faded away, replaced by a sense of playfulness and curiosity.

"Jenna, you were right!" Chris exclaimed excitedly over the phone. "I've been painting just for fun, and it's amazing. I feel like a kid again, just playing with colors and shapes."

Jenna's voice was filled with warmth, "That's fantastic, Chris! When you find your flow, the art speaks for itself. The joy you feel in the process shines through in the final piece."

Sharing the Joy

As Chris continued to embrace the creative process, he also noticed a change in his professional work. His new pieces were more vibrant and expressive, reflecting the joy he found in creating them. He decided to share his journey with his followers on social media, hoping to inspire other artists facing similar struggles.

In a video post, Chris shared, "Hey everyone, I wanted to share something personal. I've been struggling with my art lately, feeling pressured to produce and sell. But I've found joy again by focusing on the process, not the outcome. Here's a glimpse of what I've been working on just for fun."

The response was overwhelmingly positive. Fellow artists and fans alike appreciated his honesty and were inspired to reconnect with their own creative passions.

A few months later, Chris held an exhibition featuring both his professional work and the pieces he created during his personal sessions. The show was a success, with visitors commenting on the energy and emotion in his artwork.

"These pieces are incredible, Chris," one visitor remarked. "There's so much life and joy in them."

Another visitor agreed, "I can see the difference. It's like your art has a new depth and vibrancy."

Chris smiled, "Thank you. It's been a journey, but I've learned that the joy in the process is what makes the art truly come alive."

Chris's artistic breakthrough demonstrates the power of reconnecting with the intrinsic joy of creation. By prioritizing the process over the outcome, he was able to reignite his passion and rediscover the magic in his art. His story serves as a reminder that even when our passions become our profession, we can still find fulfillment and joy in embracing the creative process and allowing ourselves to simply create for the love of it.

Conclusion

Today, we've unlocked the secrets of achieving peak performance by tapping into the state of flow. We've learned that flow is more than just being "in the zone" – it's about finding that sweet spot where challenge meets skill, where time dissolves, and where you're completely absorbed in the task at hand. We discovered that finding your flow involves engaging in activities that stretch your abilities, setting clear goals, and receiving immediate feedback. By creating an environment that fosters concentration and minimizes distractions, you can regularly experience this powerful state, leading to not only enhanced productivity but also a deeper sense of satisfaction and fulfillment.

As you continue your journey, remember that the joy of the process is just as important as the outcome. Celebrate the moments when you lose yourself in your work and feel the intrinsic joy of creation and mastery. These moments are key to sustaining long-term motivation and fulfillment. Nurture your passions, embrace challenges, and allow yourself to get lost in the activities that truly ignite your soul.

Tomorrow, we'll shift our focus to igniting your professional passion and achieving career goals. Your professional life is a significant part of your overall well-being, and it's essential to find meaning, purpose, and fulfillment in your work. We'll explore how to apply the principles of self-motivation to transform your career, align your work with your deeper purpose, and achieve your career goals with renewed vigor and enthusiasm. Get ready to take your professional life to the next level!

Notes

"Your work is going to fill a large part of your life, and the only way to be truly satisfied is to do what you believe is great work. The only way to do great work is to love what you do. If you haven't found it yet, keep looking. Don't settle."

—Steve Jobs

DAY 7:
IGNITING YOUR PROFESSIONAL PASSION AND ACHIEVING CAREER GOALS

In the previous chapter, we explored the transformative power of finding your flow—that magical state of heightened focus and enjoyment that unlocks peak performance and intrinsic joy. We delved into how flow can lead to enhanced performance, increased motivation, and a deeper sense of satisfaction. Understanding how to achieve this state allows us to harness its power to elevate both our personal and professional lives. We also heard Chris's inspiring story, a testament to how reconnecting with the intrinsic joy of creation can reignite passion and creativity, even in the face of burnout.

Now, let's shift our focus to the professional realm, where we spend a significant portion of our lives. Your work can be more than just a paycheck; it can be a canvas for self-expression, a source of deep meaning and purpose, and a catalyst for personal growth. By applying the principles of self-motivation that we've been exploring, you can transform your work experience from mundane to extraordinary.

Imagine waking up each morning with a sense of excitement about the day ahead, feeling energized and passionate about your work. Picture yourself overcoming challenges with confidence, continuously learning and growing, and achieving your career goals with renewed vigor and enthusiasm. This vision is within your reach. Today, we'll explore how to align your career with your deeper purpose, ignite your professional passion, and create a fulfilling work life that fuels your motivation and brings you joy.

Reflect & Respond:

Connect with Your Purpose: What motivates you to work? Beyond financial security, what impact do you want to make through your career? Reflecting on your values, interests, and passions can help you align your work with your deeper purpose, leading to greater satisfaction and motivation.

My motivation:

_____

_____

_____

Impact I want to make:

_____

_____

_____

Set Meaningful Goals: What do you want to achieve in your career? Where do you see yourself in five or ten years? Setting clear, specific, and measurable goals can provide a roadmap for your professional journey and keep you motivated to reach new heights.

My career goals:

_____

_____

_____

My 5-10 year vision:

_____

_____

_____

Cultivate a Growth Mindset

View challenges as opportunities for learning and development. Don't be afraid to step outside your comfort zone and take on new responsibilities. View your failures as steppingstones to success and learn from your mistakes. Challenges I'm willing to embrace:

_____

_____

_____

Lessons I've learned from past failures:

_____

_____

_____

Take Ownership of Your Development

Action Plan: What are three things you can do this month to invest in your professional growth? (e.g., read a book, attend a workshop, seek out a mentor)

Build Positive Relationships

Who in your workplace inspires you or supports your growth? How can you strengthen those relationships?

Celebrate Your Wins

Action Step: List three recent accomplishments at work, no matter how small, and how you can celebrate them.

Find Joy in Your Work

What aspects of your work do you genuinely enjoy? How can you focus on those aspects more?

Maintain a Healthy Work-Life Balance

Commitment: What is one thing you can do today to improve your work-life balance? (e.g., set boundaries, schedule time off, delegate a task)

_____
_____
_____

Advocate for Yourself

Action Step: Identify one thing you need or want in your current role. How can you confidently advocate for it?

_____
_____
_____

Embrace Change

Reflection Question: How can you view upcoming changes at work as an opportunity for growth and learning?

_____
_____
_____

Igniting Your Professional Passion

When you're passionate about your work, it's no longer just a job; it's a calling. Passion fuels your drive, enhances your creativity, and inspires you to go above and beyond.

Reflect & Respond:

Rediscover Your Why: Reconnect with the reasons why you chose your career path in the first place. What excites you about it? What impact did you want to make?

_____

_____

_____

My initial reasons for choosing this career were:

Explore New Opportunities: If you're feeling stagnant, look for opportunities to learn new skills, take on new challenges, or explore different roles within your field. What actions can you take?

_____

_____

_____

Potential new opportunities I'd like to explore:

Connect with Your Values: How does your work align with your personal values? If there's a disconnect, explore ways to bridge the gap or consider alternative career paths that better reflect your values.

How my work aligns with my values:

_____

_____

_____

Potential ways to bridge the gap:

Find Meaning in Your Work: Even in seemingly mundane tasks, there's always an opportunity to find meaning and purpose. Focus on how your work contributes to the bigger picture and the positive impact you're making on others.

How my work contributes to the bigger picture:

_____

_____

_____

_____

_____

_____

_____

_____

_____

_____

_____

_____

_____

_____

Positive impact I'm making:

By engaging with these reflections and action steps, you can take charge of your professional life, rekindle your passion, and unlock your full potential for success and fulfillment.

Mark's Career Pivot: Finding Purpose in Professional Passion

Mark had been working in the finance industry for over a decade. While he was good at his job and had achieved considerable success, he couldn't shake the feeling that something was missing. The daily grind left him feeling unfulfilled, and he yearned for a career that aligned more closely with his passions and values. One evening, after a particularly long and draining day at the office, Mark met his friend, Laura, for coffee. Laura had recently made a successful career change, and Mark hoped she could offer some advice.

"Laura, I'm stuck," Mark confessed, his voice heavy with frustration. "I've been in finance for so long, but it's just not fulfilling anymore. I feel like I'm wasting my time and potential."

Laura nodded empathetically, "I get it, Mark. I was in a similar situation before I switched to non-profit work. What do you feel passionate about? What makes you excited to get out of bed in the morning?"

Mark's eyes lit up as he spoke, "I've always loved working with technology. I'm fascinated by how it can solve real-world problems and improve people's lives. But I don't know where to start. Switching careers feels so daunting."

Laura offered encouragement, "It's definitely a big step, but it's not impossible. Have you thought about what kind of roles in tech might interest you? Maybe something that combines your finance background with your passion for technology?"

Exploring New Paths

Inspired by Laura's encouragement, Mark began exploring his options. He spent the next few weeks researching various roles in the tech industry and discovered the field of fintech, where technology and finance intersect. Intrigued, he started taking online courses to build his skills in programming and data analysis. He also attended industry events and meetups to network with professionals in the field.

"Laura, I've been learning about fintech, and it's amazing!" Mark exclaimed excitedly during their next coffee date. "It's like the perfect blend of my skills and interests. I've started taking courses online, and I'm even attending some meetups to connect with people in the industry."

Laura smiled, "That's fantastic, Mark! It sounds like you're on the right track. Keep building your skills and making connections. Have you thought about reaching out to someone in the field for mentorship?"

Finding a Mentor

Taking Laura's advice, Mark reached out to James, a fintech professional he met at a networking event. James had made a similar career switch a few years ago and was eager to help.

"James, I really appreciate you taking the time to talk with me," Mark began. "I'm looking to transition into fintech and could use some guidance."

James replied, "Of course, Mark. I've been where you are. The key is to leverage your existing skills while learning new ones. Have you worked on any projects or case studies that you can showcase?"

Mark hesitated, "I've done some coursework, but I haven't applied it to real projects yet."

James offered a suggestion, "Try to build a portfolio. Even small projects can make a big difference. And don't hesitate to take on freelance work or internships to gain practical experience."

Taking the Leap

With James's mentorship and Laura's continued support, Mark dedicated himself to building his portfolio. He worked on small fintech projects, applied for internships, and gradually gained confidence in his new skills. After several months of hard work, Mark landed a role at a fintech startup, where he could finally combine his finance expertise with his passion for technology.

"Laura, I did it!" Mark exclaimed excitedly over the phone. "I got a job at a fintech startup. It feels like everything is finally coming together."

"I knew you could do it, Mark," Laura replied. "You found your passion and pursued it with determination. How does it feel?"

Mark's voice was filled with joy, "It feels incredible. I'm finally doing work that excites me and makes a difference. Thank you for all your support."

Mark's journey taught him the importance of pursuing work that aligns with his passions and values. By taking small, deliberate steps and seeking guidance from others, he was able to make a successful career pivot.

"James, I can't thank you enough for your mentorship," Mark expressed his gratitude. "This transition has been challenging, but so rewarding."

James smiled, "You've done the hard work, Mark. Remember, the journey doesn't end here. Keep learning and growing in your new role. The possibilities are endless."

Conclusion

Today, we embarked on a journey to ignite our professional passion and align our careers with our deeper purpose. We delved into the power of introspection, exploring our motivations, values, and aspirations to discover what truly brings us fulfillment in our work. By identifying our strengths, weaknesses, and areas for growth, we laid the groundwork for transforming our professional lives into a source of joy and purpose.

As you continue your transformative journey, remember that your professional life is a canvas for self-expression, a platform for personal growth, and a significant contributor to your overall well-being. By setting clear goals, seeking out opportunities for growth, and aligning your actions with your values, you can achieve lasting professional success and fulfillment.

Tomorrow, we'll tackle the inevitable challenges and obstacles that can impede our progress and motivation. We'll delve into strategies for overcoming these roadblocks, maintaining momentum, and cultivating resilience in the face of adversity. Get ready to fortify your determination and develop the tools to navigate the inevitable storms that may arise on your path to success.

Notes

PART III:
E - EMBRACE CHALLENGES AS OPPORTUNITIES

"Clutter is not just the stuff on your floor—it's anything that stands between you and the life you want to be living."

—Peter Walsh

DAY 8:
ROADBLOCKS TO RESOLVE

In the previous chapter, we embarked on a journey to ignite your professional passion and align your career goals with your deeper purpose. We explored the importance of understanding your motivations, setting meaningful goals, and embracing a growth mindset in your career. We also emphasized the significance of cultivating positive relationships, taking ownership of your professional development, and celebrating your wins. Mark's inspiring story showcased how pursuing work that aligns with your passions and values can lead to immense satisfaction and success.

Today, we'll tackle the inevitable roadblocks and challenges that can hinder your progress and motivation. The path to self-motivation is not always smooth, and we all encounter obstacles that can drain our energy, dampen our enthusiasm, and even derail our progress. But fear not, for within every challenge lies an opportunity for growth and resilience.

In this chapter, we'll shine a spotlight on some of the most common motivation killers that lurk in the shadows, ready to sabotage your journey. We'll arm you with the tools and strategies to conquer these internal foes, such as self-doubt, fear, and procrastination. By learning how to cultivate resilience and maintain momentum, you'll emerge from the storms stronger and more determined than ever to achieve your dreams. Let's transform those obstacles into steppingstones towards success!

Internal Motivation Killers

Fear of Failure: The fear of failure is a common and often crippling obstacle that can prevent us from taking risks and pursuing our goals. It can stem from various sources, such as past experiences of failure, societal pressures to succeed, or a deep-seated belief that we're not good enough. However, as Robert F. Kennedy eloquently stated, "Only those who dare to fail greatly can ever achieve greatly." This highlights the importance of embracing failure as a natural part of the learning and growth process.

Strategies

To overcome the fear of failure, consider these strategies:

- *Reframe failure as a learning opportunity*: Instead of viewing failure as a personal shortcoming, see it as a chance to learn and grow. Ask yourself, "What can I learn from this experience?" and "How can I use this feedback to improve?"
- *Embrace a growth mindset*: Believe that your abilities and intelligence can be developed through effort and perseverance. Challenges should be seen as opportunities to learn and expand your skills.
- *Focus on the process, not just the outcome*: Shift your attention from the end goal to the steps you're taking to reach it. Celebrate small victories and acknowledge the progress you're making, even if it's not perfect.
- *Start small and gradually increase the challenge*: Begin with goals that are slightly outside your comfort zone, and gradually increase the difficulty as you gain confidence.
- *Seek support*: Talk to friends, family, or a therapist about your fears and anxieties. Sharing your concerns with others can help you gain perspective and develop strategies for overcoming them.
- *Visualize success*: Imagine yourself achieving your goals and overcoming obstacles. This can help you build confidence and reduce anxiety.
- *Practice self-compassion*: Be kind to yourself when you make mistakes. Remember that everyone fails sometimes, and it's not a reflection of your worth or abilities.

Reflection

Do you often avoid taking on new challenges because you're afraid of failing? Do you tend to focus on potential negative outcomes rather than the possibility of success?

_____

_____

_____

_____

Negative Self-Talk: The relentless voice of self-doubt and criticism within us can chip away at our confidence and hinder our progress. It's crucial to remember, as a wise professor once said, "Be careful how you talk to yourself. You are always listening." This inner dialogue significantly shapes our self-perception and motivation. When negativity takes hold, it can become a self-fulfilling prophecy, preventing us from reaching our full potential.

Strategies

To combat negative self-talk, try these strategies:
- *Challenge negative thoughts*: Are they rooted in reality, or are they exaggerated fears and anxieties? Would you speak to a friend the way you speak to yourself?
- *Reframe with positive affirmations*: Replace self-deprecating thoughts with encouraging and supportive statements. For example, instead of "I can't do this," tell yourself, "I am capable and resourceful."
- *Cultivate self-compassion*: Remember that everyone makes mistakes. Treat yourself with kindness and understanding, just as you would a friend.
- *Focus on solutions*: Instead of dwelling on what's wrong, direct your energy towards finding solutions and learning from setbacks.

- ***Seek support***: Talk to a trusted friend, family member, therapist, or mentor who can offer encouragement and perspective.

Reflection

What are some common negative thoughts that pop up in your mind? How do these thoughts affect your mood and motivation? What positive affirmations can you use to counteract these negative thoughts? What steps can you take to cultivate self-compassion and silence your inner critic?

___

___

___

___

Perfectionism: The relentless pursuit of flawlessness can be a significant roadblock to motivation. It can lead to procrastination, anxiety, and a crippling fear of failure. Striving for excellence is admirable, but when it becomes an obsession with unattainable perfection, it can paralyze us and hinder our progress.

Strategies

To overcome the trap of perfectionism, consider these strategies:
- ***Reframe your expectations***: Are your standards realistic and attainable? Are you holding yourself to a higher standard than you would hold others? Strive for excellence, not perfection.
- ***Shift your focus***: Instead of fixating on flaws and mistakes, focus on your progress and accomplishments. Celebrate every step forward, no matter how small.

- ***Embrace imperfection***: Recognize that mistakes are a natural part of the learning process. Learn from your setbacks and use them as opportunities to grow.
- ***Practice self-compassion***: Be kind to yourself. Don't beat yourself up over imperfections or setbacks. Instead, treat yourself with the same understanding and compassion you would offer a friend.
- ***Set realistic goals***: Break down large tasks into smaller, more manageable steps. This will help you make progress and feel a sense of accomplishment along the way.
- ***Invest in yourself through self-care***: Carve out time for activities that nourish your mind, body, and spirit, fueling your overall resilience and happiness. This will help you reduce stress and maintain a healthy perspective.

Reflection

What are the costs and benefits of my perfectionism? What would my life look like if I embraced imperfection? How can I shift my focus from perfection to progress? What steps can I take to practice self-compassion? How can I set more realistic expectations for myself?

_____

_____

_____

_____

Burnout: The relentless grind of chronic stress and overwork can leave you feeling utterly depleted, both physically and emotionally. It's like a slow leak in your motivation reserves, leaving you feeling disillusioned and disengaged from the things that once brought you joy and fulfillment.

Strategies

Here are some strategies to combat burnout:

- **Prioritize rest and relaxation**: Get enough sleep, take breaks throughout the day, and engage in activities that help you unwind and de-stress.
- **Set boundaries**: Learn to say no to additional commitments or responsibilities when you're feeling overwhelmed.
- **Delegate tasks**: Don't try to do everything yourself. Delegate tasks to others or ask for help when needed.
- **Connect with others**: Spend time with loved ones, engage in social activities, and build a support system.
- **Re-evaluate your priorities**: Are your current commitments aligned with your values and goals? If not, make adjustments to create a more fulfilling and sustainable lifestyle.
- **Seek professional help**: If you're struggling to cope with burnout on your own, don't hesitate to seek help from a therapist or counselor.

Reflection

Have you lost interest in or enthusiasm for activities you once enjoyed? Do you feel like you're merely going through the motions, lacking any sense of accomplishment or satisfaction? Are you experiencing physical symptoms like fatigue, headaches, or digestive issues? Do you find yourself becoming increasingly cynical, irritable, or detached?

_____

_____

_____

_____

If these resonate with you, it's crucial to prioritize self-care and set boundaries to replenish your energy and reignite your motivation. Burnout isn't a badge of honor; it's a sign that you need to recharge.

External Motivation Killers

Procrastination: Procrastination often tricks us into believing it's a strategic way to work, a common misconception that I personally fell prey to in college. I convinced myself that waiting until the last minute to write papers would somehow magically enhance my productivity and creativity. However, the reality was quite the opposite. The pressure of looming deadlines only amplified my stress and anxiety, hindering my ability to produce my best work.

As Mason Cooley aptly put it, "Procrastination makes easy things hard, hard things harder." This quote perfectly encapsulates the vicious cycle of procrastination, where the initial delay only exacerbates the difficulty of the task, leading to further procrastination and increased stress.

Strategies

To break free from this counterproductive pattern, try these strategies:

- ***Identify your triggers***: What emotions or thoughts do you experience when you think about starting a task you've been procrastinating on? Are you feeling overwhelmed, anxious, or bored? Recognizing these triggers can help you develop coping mechanisms and preemptive strategies.
- ***Break down large tasks***: Divide daunting projects into smaller, more manageable steps. This will make the task seem less overwhelming and provide a sense of accomplishment as you complete each step.
- ***Set deadlines and create a schedule***: Establish clear deadlines for each step and create a realistic schedule to keep yourself accountable and on track.

- ***Reward yourself for progress***: Celebrate your achievements, no matter how small. This positive reinforcement can help you stay motivated and build momentum.
- ***Eliminate distractions***: Minimize distractions by turning off notifications, silencing your phone, and creating a dedicated workspace.
- ***Start with the easiest task***: Sometimes, the hardest part is simply getting started. Begin with a small, easy task to get the ball rolling and build momentum.

Reflection

Do you notice any patterns in your procrastination habits? Are there certain types of tasks or situations that you tend to put off more than others? Understanding your procrastination tendencies can help you tailor these strategies to your specific needs and overcome this common motivation killer.

_____

_____

_____

_____

Lack of Clarity: When our goals are vague or undefined, it's like trying to navigate a maze without a map or compass. We may start with enthusiasm, but without a clear direction, our motivation can quickly fizzle out, leaving us feeling lost and aimless. Setting SMART goals provides a clear roadmap for our journey, allowing us to track our progress and stay focused on what truly matters.

Reflection

What are my long-term aspirations? Where do I see myself in the next 5-10 years? What specific steps can I take to move closer to these aspirations? How can I break down my long-term goals into smaller, more manageable short-term goals? What resources or support do I need to achieve these goals? How will I measure my progress and know when I've achieved my goals?

By answering these questions and setting SMART goals, you can create a clear path forward, reignite your motivation, and stay on track even when faced with challenges or setbacks. Remember to revisit your goals regularly to ensure they are still relevant and aligned with your values and aspirations.

Lack of Support: We all need encouragement and support to stay motivated, especially when facing challenges or setbacks. Feeling isolated or unsupported can drain our energy and make it difficult to persevere. As I discovered when I invited my friend Laura to join a local book writing group, connecting with like-minded individuals can be incredibly empowering. Surrounding yourself with a supportive community can provide valuable guidance, accountability, and encouragement, reminding you that you're not alone in your struggles and aspirations.

Reflection

If you're feeling a lack of support, consider these questions:

What specific areas of my life would I like to receive more support in? Identifying your specific needs can help you determine the type of support that would be most beneficial.

_____

_____

_____

_____

What kind of support am I looking for? Are you seeking emotional support, practical advice, or a combination of both? Do you prefer one-on-one mentorship, group support, or online communities?

_____

_____

_____

_____

Where can I find support groups or communities that align with my interests and needs? Look for online directories, local community centers, or organizations related to your field or personal interests. There are numerous online forums and social media groups dedicated to various topics and interests.

_____

_____

_____

_____

How can I reach out to potential mentors or coaches? Consider professionals in your field, experienced individuals you admire, or even friends and family members who have expertise in areas you want to develop.

_____

_____

What qualities am I looking for in a mentor or support group? Are you looking for someone who is knowledgeable, empathetic, encouraging, or challenging? Identifying your preferences can help you find the right fit.

___

Remember, creating a support system is a journey, not a sprint. Be patient with yourself and remember that reaching out for help is a sign of strength, not weakness. You might be surprised at how many people are willing to offer their support and encouragement. By connecting with others who share your passions and goals, you can create a powerful network that fuels your motivation and propels you towards success.

Comparisonitis: The curated highlight reels that dominate social media can easily lead us down a path of self-doubt and comparison, making it difficult to appreciate our own unique journeys. This "comparisonitis," as aptly described by Theodore Roosevelt, can rob us of the joy found in our own unique journey. When we constantly measure ourselves against others, we often focus on our perceived shortcomings, fueling feelings of inadequacy and envy that can ultimately sabotage our motivation.

Reflection

To break free from the comparison trap and cultivate a healthier relationship with yourself, consider these questions:

What triggers my comparison tendencies? Is it specific individuals, social media platforms, certain situations, or internal thoughts? By identifying your triggers, you can develop strategies to manage and minimize their impact.

___

___

___

___

Am I comparing my behind-the-scenes to someone else's highlight reel? Remember, social media often presents a distorted view of reality. People typically share their successes and best moments, not their struggles or failures. Don't compare your everyday life to someone else's carefully curated online persona.

___

___

___

___

What are my unique strengths and accomplishments? Shift your focus inward and take stock of your own abilities, skills, and achievements. What makes you unique and valuable?

_____

_____

_____

_____

How can I use comparison as a source of inspiration rather than discouragement? Instead of feeling envious, let the achievements of others inspire and motivate you to reach your own goals. How can their success serve as a model or roadmap for your own journey?

_____

_____

_____

_____

How can I focus on my own progress and growth? Celebrate your own milestones, no matter how small they may seem. Track your progress over time and acknowledge the effort and dedication you've put into your journey.

_____

_____

_____

_____

Remember, everyone's path is different, and your journey is just as valid and worthy of celebration as anyone else's. By focusing on your own unique strengths and accomplishments, you can cultivate a sense of self-worth and confidence that will propel you forward, regardless of what others are doing.

Distractions: In today's hyper-connected world, distractions are a constant threat to our focus and productivity. From the alluring ping of a new notification to the endless stream of emails flooding our inboxes, it's easy to lose sight of our goals and get sidetracked. However, by recognizing these distractions and implementing strategies to minimize their impact, we can reclaim our focus and maximize our productivity.

Reflection

To create a distraction-free environment and harness your focus, consider these questions:

What are my biggest distractions? Are they external, like social media or noisy environments, or internal, like wandering thoughts or worries? Identifying your specific distractions is the first step to overcoming them.

_____

_____

_____

_____

What time of day am I most productive? Are you a morning person or a night owl? Schedule your most challenging tasks during your peak focus times to maximize your efficiency and output.

_____

_____

_____

_____

How can I design my workspace to minimize distractions ? Can you declutter your desk, turn off notifications, or use noise-canceling headphones ?

_____

_____

_____

_____

What tools or apps can I use to block distracting websites and apps? There are numerous tools available that can help you limit your access to time-wasting websites and apps during designated work periods.

_____

_____

_____

_____

How can I incorporate regular breaks into my schedule? Taking short breaks throughout the day can actually improve focus and prevent burnout.

_____

_____

_____

_____

What self-care practices can I implement to improve my focus? Prioritize sleep, exercise, and healthy eating to optimize your cognitive function and reduce mental fatigue.

_____

_____

_____

_____

By answering these questions and implementing these strategies, you can create a more focused and productive work environment, allowing you to tackle your goals with renewed energy and determination. Remember, distractions are inevitable, but with the right mindset and tools, you can minimize their impact and stay on track.

Lack of Meaning: Feeling a lack of purpose or meaning can leave us adrift, lacking the drive and direction that fuel motivation. When our actions feel disconnected from our deeper values and passions, it's easy to lose interest and enthusiasm. To reignite your motivation, it's essential to reconnect with what truly matters to you and find activities that align with your values and give you a sense of fulfillment.

Reflection

Here are some questions to help you explore your sense of meaning and purpose:

What activities or causes make you feel most alive and engaged? When do you feel a sense of flow or excitement? What kind of work or hobbies make you lose track of time?

_____

_____

_____

_____

What are your core values and beliefs? What principles guide your decisions and actions? What kind of world do you want to live in, and how can you contribute to that vision?

_____

_____

_____

_____

What are your unique strengths and talents? How can you use your skills and abilities to make a difference in the world or contribute to something meaningful?

_____

_____

_____

_____

What problems or challenges in the world resonate with you? Are there any causes or issues that you feel strongly about and want to be a part of the solution for?

_____

_____

_____

_____

What kind of legacy do you want to leave behind? How do you want to be remembered by others? What kind of positive impact do you want to have on the world?

_____

_____

_____

_____

Reflecting on these questions can help you clarify your values, passions, and purpose. Once you have a better understanding of what truly matters to you, you can start to make choices and take actions that align with those values. This alignment can create a profound sense of meaning and purpose, which in turn fuels your motivation and drives you toward your goals.

Even small steps can make a big difference. What one small action can you take today to start living a more purposeful life? It could be as simple as volunteering your time for a cause you care about, starting a new hobby that brings you joy, or simply setting aside time each day for reflection and gratitude. Remember, finding meaning and purpose is an ongoing journey, not a destination. It requires constant self-reflection and a willingness to explore new possibilities.

Anna's Fitness Routine: Small Habits, Big Changes

Anna had always struggled with maintaining a consistent fitness routine. She would start with enthusiasm, only to lose motivation after a few weeks. Her busy schedule as a marketing executive left her feeling exhausted and overwhelmed by the end of each day. Yet she knew that staying active was essential for her physical and mental well-being. One evening, after a particularly stressful day, she decided to call her friend, Mia, a fitness coach, for some advice.

"Mia, I'm really struggling to stick to a fitness routine," Anna confessed, frustration evident in her voice. "I start strong but always end up quitting. I feel like I just don't have the time or energy."

Mia responded with understanding, "I hear you, Anna. It's tough to balance everything. But the key is to start small and build from there. You don't need to overhaul your life overnight. Let's break it down into manageable steps."

Anna was curious, "What do you mean by starting small? Like, how small?"

Mia explained, "Even just a few minutes a day. The goal is to create small, sustainable habits that become part of your daily routine. Once these habits are in place, you can gradually increase the intensity and duration."

Setting Small Goals
Taking Mia's advice to heart, Anna decided to start with a simple goal: a 10-minute walk every morning. It seemed almost too easy, but Mia assured her that consistency was more important than intensity at this stage.

"Remember, Anna, it's about creating a habit," Mia emphasized. "Set a time each day for your walk and stick to it. Don't worry about the distance or speed right now. Just get moving."

Anna nodded in agreement, "Okay, I can do that. Ten minutes doesn't seem too daunting."

Building Momentum
Anna began her new routine the next morning. She set her alarm 15 minutes earlier, put on her walking shoes, and headed out the door. The fresh air and quiet morning helped clear her mind and set a positive tone for the day. After a week, she found herself looking forward to her walks.

"Mia, you were right," Anna said with a smile. "I actually enjoy these morning walks. They give me a good start to the day."

Mia was pleased to hear it, "I'm glad to hear that! Now that you've established this habit, let's add another small goal. How about some light stretching or yoga after your walk?"

Anna agreed, "Sure, that sounds doable. I'll give it a try."

Adding to the Routine
Over the next few weeks, Anna incorporated a 10-minute stretching session after her walks. She felt more energized and less stressed, and the

physical activity began to feel like a natural part of her day. Encouraged by her progress, she decided to add a short workout session twice a week.

"Mia, I've been doing the walks and stretching, and I feel great," Anna reported. "I think I'm ready to add some more exercise. What do you suggest?"

"That's fantastic, Anna!" Mia exclaimed. "Let's start with a 20-minute strength training session twice a week. Focus on basic exercises like squats, lunges, and push-ups. Keep it simple and listen to your body."

Embracing the Changes
Anna followed Mia's plan, and soon her fitness routine became a series of small, manageable habits. She found that by breaking her goals into smaller steps, she could maintain consistency without feeling overwhelmed. Her energy levels increased, and she noticed positive changes in her physical and mental health.

"Mia, I can't believe how much better I feel," Anna exclaimed. "These small changes have made a big difference. I'm not just sticking to my routine; I'm enjoying it."

Mia replied, "That's the power of small habits, Anna. They build up over time and lead to significant changes. I'm so proud of you for sticking with it."

Anna's journey to establishing a fitness routine taught her the value of small, consistent habits. By starting with manageable goals and gradually building on them, she transformed her approach to fitness and made it a sustainable part of her life.

"Thank you, Mia," Anna expressed her gratitude. "Your advice has been a game-changer. I've learned that it's not about making huge changes overnight but about small steps that lead to big results."

Mia smiled, "You're welcome, Anna. I'm glad I could help. Remember, it's about enjoying the journey and taking it one step at a time."

Conclusion

Today, we delved into the concept of overcoming roadblocks and cultivating resilience. We explored various internal motivation killers and identified strategies to tackle them effectively. By recognizing and addressing self-doubt, fear, and procrastination, you can build the resilience needed to stay focused and motivated in the face of adversity. The story of Anna's fitness routine demonstrated the power of setting small, achievable goals and building momentum over time, leading to significant changes and lasting motivation.

As you continue your journey, remember that setbacks are a natural part of the process. Embrace them as opportunities for growth and learning. By developing a resilient mindset, you can overcome any challenge that comes your way and stay on track towards your goals.

Tomorrow, we'll delve deeper into the concept of resilience and explore how to turn obstacles into opportunities. We'll discuss the importance of a growth mindset and how to stay motivated during tough times. Get ready to learn practical strategies for maintaining your motivation and turning setbacks into comebacks. Let's continue this journey with renewed determination and a resilient spirit.

Notes

"The oak fought the wind and was broken, the willow bent when it must and survived."

—Robert Jordan

DAY 9:
OVERCOMING OBSTACLES TO STAY MOTIVATED

In the previous chapter, we delved into the myriad roadblocks that can derail our motivation and hinder our progress. We explored both internal and external obstacles, such as fear of failure, negative self-talk, and a lack of support, and learned practical strategies to overcome these challenges. We also heard Anna's inspiring story of how she transformed her fitness routine by setting small, manageable goals and building momentum through consistent action.

Today, we'll take our understanding of obstacles a step further by focusing on how to stay motivated in the face of adversity. The path to success is rarely a straight line; it's often riddled with unexpected twists and turns, uphill battles, and seemingly insurmountable obstacles. Even the most motivated individuals will face setbacks, disappointments, and moments of doubt. But it's how we respond to these challenges that ultimately determine our success. By embracing setbacks as opportunities for growth and developing resilience, we can maintain our motivation and continue moving forward, no matter what challenges arise. Let's dive in and explore effective strategies for turning setbacks into comebacks and maintaining our drive in the face of adversity.

Embracing the Inevitable: Obstacles as Opportunities

Think of a time when you faced a major challenge in your life. How did it feel? Did you give up, or did you find a way to overcome it? The first step to overcoming obstacles is to accept that they are an inevitable part of life. No matter how well we plan or how hard we work, there will be roadblocks along the way. Instead of viewing obstacles as setbacks, reframe them as opportunities for growth and learning[21]. Each challenge you overcome strengthens your resilience, builds your character, and brings you one step closer to your goals.

Time Management Strategies

In the pursuit of our dreams, taking consistent action is key. However, the demands of daily life often leave us wondering, "How can I find the time to chase my dreams?" If you struggle with carving out precious moments to dedicate to your aspirations, you're not alone. Today, we'll explore not only the importance of taking action but also practical strategies for effectively managing your time to ensure those actions propel you toward your goals.

The Power of Action

Remember, action is the bridge between your dreams and reality. It's about moving beyond planning and visualization and taking tangible steps toward your goals. Even small actions can create a ripple effect, leading to significant progress over time. So, start small, build momentum, and celebrate each victory along the way.

Mastering Time Management

I recently revisited a classic article in the Harvard Business Review titled "Management Time: Who's Got the Monkey?" It explores a common challenge faced by managers: feeling overwhelmed by an abundance of problems, often those of their subordinates. The article uses the metaphor of monkeys jumping onto the manager's back, signifying the transfer of responsibility when an employee brings a problem to their manager.

---

21 Ryan Holiday, *The Obstacle Is the Way: The Timeless Art of Turning Trials into Triumph*, 1st ed. (n.p.: Portfolio, 2014).

Although the article primarily focuses on managers and delegating tasks, it offers a valuable lesson applicable to our personal lives: the importance of recognizing when we've taken on too much. In the pursuit of our dreams, we often find ourselves juggling numerous responsibilities and commitments, leaving us feeling overwhelmed and stressed. It's as if we're carrying a multitude of metaphorical monkeys on our backs, each one representing a task, worry, or obligation.

Just as an overburdened manager struggles to prioritize and complete tasks efficiently, so too can we become bogged down by an excess of "monkeys" in our personal lives. It's essential to learn how to manage these responsibilities effectively and avoid taking on more than we can handle. This might involve prioritizing tasks, delegating when possible, learning to say no, or seeking support from others.

Just as the article advises managers to empower their subordinates, we must also empower ourselves to take control of our time and energy. This involves setting boundaries, prioritizing self-care, and making conscious choices about how we allocate our resources. By learning to manage our "monkeys" effectively, we can free up more time and energy to focus on what truly matters—our dreams and aspirations. Remember, we are the authors of our own stories, and it's up to us to ensure that those stories are filled with joy, fulfillment, and the pursuit of our passions.

Strategies for Overcoming Obstacles

Effective time management is crucial for achieving your goals. Here are some strategies to overcome common time management obstacles:

- Prioritize: Identify your most important tasks and focus on them first. Don't get bogged down by less urgent matters.
- Set Realistic Goals: Break down large goals into smaller, more manageable tasks. This makes them less daunting and more achievable.

- Schedule Your Time: Create a daily or weekly schedule and allocate specific time slots for different activities. This helps you stay organized and focused.
- Avoid Distractions: Minimize distractions like social media, emails, and unnecessary interruptions during your dedicated work periods.
- Take Breaks: Short breaks can actually boost productivity. Step away from your work for a few minutes to recharge and refocus.
- Delegate: If possible, delegate tasks that others can handle, freeing up your time for more important matters.
- Learn to Say No: Don't overcommit yourself. Be selective about the tasks and projects you take on to avoid burnout.
- Use Time Management Tools: Explore a variety of time management apps and tools to help you stay organized and track your progress.

Remember, time management is a skill that takes practice and discipline. By implementing these strategies and making conscious choices about how you spend your time, you can overcome obstacles, stay focused, and make significant strides towards achieving your dreams.

Overcoming Procrastination and Self-Doubt

Procrastination and self-doubt can be formidable roadblocks on your journey toward achieving your dreams. Research has shown that these two psychological phenomena are often intertwined, with self-doubt fueling procrastination and procrastination, in turn reinforcing feelings of inadequacy.

Recent research has shed light on the connection between procrastination and self-doubt[22]. Studies have shown that individuals who struggle with self-doubt tend to put things off more often. This suggests that procrastination might be a way to avoid the fear of messing up or being judged.

---

22 Anas Awwad et al., "Procrastination in Daily Academic Tasks and Its Relationship to Self-Esteem Among University Students," *International journal of health sciences* (2022), https://doi.org/10.53730/ijhs.v6ns6.10981.

It's like a bit of a catch-22: self-doubt fuels procrastination, and then procrastination makes you doubt yourself even more[23]. But don't worry, there's good news! Both procrastination and self-doubt can be tackled head-on. By understanding what's behind them and using some helpful tips, you can break free from these patterns and start feeling more confident.

In the next few sections, we'll dive into some practical ways to beat procrastination and boost your self-belief. We'll give you the tools to take charge of your time, overcome obstacles, and finally achieve those dreams you've been putting off. Here are some tips to overcome them:

- Identify the Root Cause: Understand why you procrastinate. Are you afraid of failure? Do you feel overwhelmed by the task? Once you know the cause, you can address it.
- Start Small: If a task seems daunting, break it down into smaller, more manageable steps. Take that first small step to get the ball rolling.
- Set Deadlines: Give yourself a deadline for each task and hold yourself accountable.
- Reward Yourself: Celebrate your accomplishments, no matter how small. This positive reinforcement will motivate you to keep going.
- Challenge Negative Self-Talk: Silence the inner critic by actively affirming your worth and potential. Remind yourself of the challenges you've overcome and the goals you've achieved to nurture a more optimistic outlook.

Remember, everyone experiences procrastination and self-doubt at times. The key is to recognize these feelings and develop strategies to overcome them. Don't let them derail your progress.

Now, armed with these time management strategies and tools to overcome procrastination and self-doubt, you are ready to take massive action towards your dreams!

---

23 Saeed Ghasempour et al., "Relationship between Academic Procrastination, Self-Esteem, and Moral Intelligence Among Medical Sciences Students: A Cross-Sectional Study," *BMC Psychology* 12, no. 1 (2024), https://doi.org/10.1186/s40359-024-01731-8.

Navigating the Storm: Strategies for Overcoming Obstacles

The path to realizing our dreams is rarely a smooth one. Obstacles and setbacks are inevitable, but how we respond to them can make all the difference. In this section, we'll delve deeper into understanding the root causes of your challenges, empowering you to transform setbacks into steppingstones. Remember, every obstacle presents an opportunity for growth and learning. Let's explore some key questions that can help you uncover the source of your challenges and pave the way for a smoother journey towards your dreams.

Identify the Root Cause:
Reflection Question: What is the underlying issue behind this obstacle? Is it a lack of resources, knowledge, skill, or support?

_____

_____

_____

_____

Break Down the Problem:
Action Step: List the smaller steps needed to tackle this obstacle. What's the very first action you can take?

_____

_____

_____

_____

Seek Help and Support:

Brainstorm: Who in your network could offer support or advice? Are there any relevant groups or communities you could join?

_____

_____

_____

_____

Reframe Your Perspective:

Challenge: Can you identify three potential positive outcomes or opportunities that could arise from this obstacle?

_____

_____

_____

_____

Practice Self-Compassion:

Affirmation: Write a few kind and encouraging words to yourself, acknowledging your efforts and reminding yourself of your strengths.

_____

_____

_____

_____

Celebrate Small Wins:
Reward: What small reward can you give yourself for each step you take towards overcoming this obstacle?

_____

_____

_____

_____

Focus on What You Can Control:
Action Step: List the aspects of this situation that are within your control. What actions can you take today to move forward?

_____

_____

_____

_____

Learn from Your Mistakes:
Reflection Question: What have you learned from past challenges that you can apply to this current situation?

_____

_____

_____

_____

Focus on the Positives:
Gratitude Practice: Write down three things you are grateful for in your life right now.

_____

_____

_____

_____

Remember, obstacles are not roadblocks; they're steppingstones on the path to success. By reflecting on these questions and taking the suggested actions, you equip yourself with the tools to navigate any storm. Embrace the challenges, learn from them, and allow them to propel you forward. With the right mindset and strategies, you can overcome any obstacle and emerge stronger, wiser, and closer to achieving your wildest dreams.

Maya's Entrepreneurial Journey: Turning Setbacks into Comebacks

Maya had always dreamed of starting her own business. After years of working for others, she finally took the leap and launched her own start-up, a tech company aimed at developing innovative solutions for remote work. The initial response was positive, and she managed to secure some early investors. However, as time went on, she faced numerous challenges that threatened to derail her dreams.

One evening, feeling particularly defeated after a major setback, Maya called her mentor, Alex, an experienced entrepreneur who had faced his share of obstacles.

"Alex, I don't know what to do," Maya confessed, her voice filled with frustration. "We just lost a major client, and our latest product update has been delayed again. I feel like everything is falling apart."

Alex responded calmly, "I understand, Maya. It's tough, but setbacks are part of the journey. The important thing is how you respond to them. Let's break it down and figure out a way forward."

The First Setback

Maya explained how they lost a major client due to a competitor offering a similar product at a lower price. It was a significant blow to her confidence and the company's financial stability.

"We worked so hard on this product, and to lose a client like this… it feels like a failure," Maya lamented.

Alex reassured her, "It's not a failure, Maya. It's a learning opportunity. What can we learn from this? Can we improve our product or adjust our pricing strategy to stay competitive?"

Maya, after a moment of thought, replied, "Maybe we need to focus more on what sets us apart. Our product has unique features that we haven't marketed well. And perhaps we can find ways to offer more flexible pricing options."

The Product Delay

Next, Maya discussed the ongoing delays with their product update. Technical issues and miscommunications within the team were causing significant setbacks.

"The delays are killing us," Maya admitted. "Our team is demoralized, and I'm worried we'll lose more clients if we can't deliver on time."

Alex inquired, "Delays happen, especially with tech products. Have you identified the root cause of the delays? Is it a technical issue, or is there a breakdown in communication?"

Maya sighed, "It's a bit of both. We're having some technical difficulties, but I think a lot of it comes down to poor communication within the team."

Alex offered guidance, "Then that's where you need to focus. Clear communication and setting realistic timelines are crucial. Have a team meeting, address the issues openly, and work together to find solutions. Empower your team to take ownership of their tasks and support each other."

Turning Setbacks into Comebacks

With Alex's advice, Maya called a team meeting the next day. She openly discussed the challenges they were facing and encouraged everyone to share their thoughts and suggestions.

"I know things have been tough lately," Maya began, "but I believe in this team and our vision. Let's talk about what's been going wrong and how we can fix it together."

One team member spoke up, "I think we need more regular check-ins to ensure everyone is on the same page. Sometimes, we don't realize there's a problem until it's too late."

Another team member agreed, "Also, maybe we can break down the tasks into smaller milestones. That way, we can catch issues early and adjust as needed."

Maya nodded, "Great ideas. Let's implement more frequent check-ins and set smaller milestones for the project. We'll also work on improving our communication channels. I'm confident we can turn this around."

With renewed focus and a clear plan, the team began making progress. They fixed the technical issues, improved their communication, and started hitting their new milestones. Slowly but surely, they regained their momentum.

A few months later, Maya's company was back on track. They regained their clients' trust and even attracted new ones with their improved product and competitive pricing. Maya learned that setbacks were not the end but an opportunity to learn, adapt, and grow.

"Alex, I can't thank you enough," Maya expressed her gratitude. "Your advice helped me see things differently. We've turned things around, and the team is more motivated than ever."

Alex smiled. "I'm glad to hear that, Maya. Remember, setbacks are just steppingstones. Every challenge is a chance to improve and come back stronger."

Conclusion

Today, we focused on the inevitable challenges that can impede our progress and explored strategies for maintaining motivation in the face of adversity. We learned that obstacles, rather than being roadblocks, can serve as opportunities for growth and resilience. By adopting a positive mindset, seeking support, and employing practical techniques to overcome setbacks, we can keep our motivation alive and continue moving towards our goals.

Tomorrow, we'll shift our focus to the importance of building and strengthening relationships through self-motivation. We'll explore how our drive and determination can positively impact those around us and how creating a supportive network can enhance our journey. Get ready to learn about the ripple effect of self-motivation and how it can foster deeper connections and mutual growth.

PART IV:
A - ASSEMBLE YOUR SUPPORT NETWORK

"Flow is being completely involved in an activity for its own sake. The ego falls away. Time flies. Every action, movement, and thought follows inevitably from the previous one, like playing jazz. Your whole being is involved, and you're using your skills to the utmost."

—Mihaly Csikszentmihalyi

DAY 10:
STRENGTHENING RELATIONSHIPS THROUGH SELF-MOTIVATION

In the previous chapter, we focused on the crucial skill of overcoming obstacles and maintaining motivation in the face of adversity. We explored how to turn setbacks into comebacks by embracing challenges as opportunities for growth and developing resilience. By adopting a positive mindset, seeking support, and employing practical techniques to overcome setbacks, we learned how to keep our motivation alive and continue moving towards our goals, no matter what challenges arise.

Today, we'll shift our focus to the powerful impact of self-motivation on our relationships. Our personal drive and determination not only propel us forward but also significantly influence those around us. Just as a pebble tossed into a pond creates ripples that extend outward, our self-motivation can create a positive ripple effect in our relationships, fostering deeper connections, mutual growth, and a more fulfilling social environment.

Nurturing Connections: Strategies for Building Stronger Bonds

Our relationships with others are essential for our happiness, well-being, and overall success. They provide love, support, and companionship, enriching our lives in countless ways. However, relationships are not static; they are dynamic connections that require nurturing and attention to thrive. By applying the principles of self-motivation to our relationships, we can strengthen our bonds with loved ones, improve communication, and create more fulfilling and harmonious connections. Let's embark on this journey to discover how our inner drive can transform our relationships and enrich our lives.

Reflection: Take a moment to reflect: When was the last time you truly connected with someone you cared about? Did you engage in an activity you both enjoy or simply share a heartfelt conversation?

_____

_____

_____

_____

Make a conscious effort to carve out quality time for your loved ones, free from distractions and obligations. Be fully present in the moment, actively listening to their words and understanding their underlying emotions and needs.

Open and honest communication is the cornerstone of any strong relationship. Share your thoughts, feelings, and needs with your loved ones in a clear and respectful manner, creating a safe space for them to do the same. Be open to feedback, willing to compromise, and avoid bottling up emotions or resorting to passive-aggressive behavior.

Appreciation and gratitude are the currencies of love and connection. Express your gratitude to the people in your life, letting them know how much you value their presence and the positive impact they have on you. A simple "thank you" can go a long way in strengthening bonds and fostering a deeper sense of connection. Remember, everyone loves to hear their own name and feel appreciated for their unique contributions.

Forgiveness is a powerful act of healing and growth. Holding onto grudges or past hurts can poison a relationship, creating a barrier to intimacy and connection. Practice forgiveness, both for yourself and others. Let go of resentment and focus on building a positive future together.

Self-Motivation's Ripple Effect

Your personal motivation plays a crucial role in your relationships. When you're motivated and engaged in life, you radiate positive energy and enthusiasm, which naturally spills over into your interactions with others. You're more likely to be supportive, encouraging, and present, creating a ripple effect that strengthens your bonds and fosters a more fulfilling relationship dynamic.

Furthermore, self-motivation empowers you to set healthy boundaries and communicate your needs effectively. When you understand your own values and priorities, you can better navigate relationships in a way that is mutually respectful and supportive.

Remember, relationships are a continuous journey of connection, growth, and self-discovery. By investing in your own self-motivation and applying these principles to your interactions with others, you can create deeper, more meaningful relationships that enrich your life and bring lasting joy.

Elena's Connection Quest: Building Stronger Bonds

Elena was a successful marketing manager, known for her dedication and hard work. However, she often felt isolated and disconnected from her colleagues and friends. Despite her professional success, her personal relationships lacked depth and connection. One evening, after a long day at the office, she confided in her friend, Mia, over a cup of coffee.

"Mia, I feel so disconnected from everyone," Elena sighed, her voice tinged with sadness. "I spend so much time at work that I hardly have time for my friends and family. Even at work, my relationships with colleagues are so superficial."

Mia nodded understandingly, "I get it, Elena. It's easy to get caught up in work and lose sight of our personal connections. But it's never too late to rebuild those bonds. Have you thought about ways to strengthen your relationships?"

Elena admitted, "I want to, but I'm not sure where to start. It feels overwhelming to make time for everything."

Mia offered a gentle suggestion, "Start small. Focus on being present and making meaningful connections in little ways. Sometimes, it's the small gestures that make the biggest difference."

Taking Small Steps

Encouraged by Mia's advice, Elena decided to take small steps to reconnect with her loved ones and build stronger bonds. She began by setting aside time each week to catch up with friends and family, whether it was a quick phone call, a video chat, or a weekend brunch. She also made a conscious effort to engage more deeply with her colleagues, asking about their lives outside of work and sharing her own experiences.

"Mia, I've started setting aside time every week to connect with friends and family," Elena reported during their next coffee date. "It's been nice to reconnect. I've also been trying to be more present at work, asking colleagues about their lives outside of work and sharing my own experiences."

Mia smiled, "That's great, Elena! How's it going so far?"

Elena's face lit up, "It's going well. I've had some really meaningful conversations. It feels good to connect on a deeper level."

Building Workplace Relationships

At work, Elena decided to organize regular team lunches and coffee breaks to foster a sense of camaraderie among her colleagues. She also initiated a monthly team-building activity where everyone could unwind and get to know each other better.

"Hey team," Elena announced during a meeting, "I was thinking we could start having lunch together once a week. It'll be a good way to take a break and get to know each other better."

"That sounds like a great idea, Elena," one colleague chimed in. "I'd love to join."

Another colleague agreed, "Count me in too. It'll be nice to have some time to chat outside of work."

Elena continued, "Awesome! I was also thinking we could do a fun team-building activity once a month. Maybe something like a cooking class or an escape room. What do you think?"

"I love that idea!" another colleague exclaimed. "It'll be a great way to bond as a team."

Rekindling Friendships

Elena also reached out to old friends she had lost touch with over the years. She scheduled regular coffee dates and catch-up sessions, rekindling friendships that had faded due to her busy schedule.

"Hi, Sarah! It's been ages," Elena said over the phone. "How have you been? I'd love to catch up over coffee sometime."

Sarah's voice was filled with warmth, "Elena! It's so good to hear from you. I've been well. Coffee sounds great. How about this Saturday?"

"Perfect!" Elena replied. "Let's meet at our old favorite spot."

Creating Deeper Connections

As Elena continued to make these small efforts, she noticed a significant improvement in her relationships. Her conversations became more meaningful, and she felt more connected to the people around her. She realized that strengthening relationships wasn't about grand gestures but about being present, listening, and showing genuine interest in others.

"How's your connection quest going, Elena?" Mia inquired during their next meet-up.

Elena smiled, "It's going really well, Mia. I've had some amazing conversations and built stronger bonds with my colleagues and friends. It feels good to be more connected."

Mia nodded approvingly, "I'm so happy to hear that. Remember, relationships are like plants. They need regular care and attention to grow."

Elena's journey taught her the importance of prioritizing relationships and making small, consistent efforts to connect with others. By being present and showing genuine interest, she was able to build stronger, more meaningful bonds.

"Thank you for your advice, Mia," Elena expressed her gratitude. "It's made such a difference in my life. I feel more connected and fulfilled."

Mia smiled, "I'm glad I could help, Elena. Keep nurturing those relationships. They're one of the most valuable parts of life."

Conclusion

Today, we explored how self-motivation can strengthen relationships and create a positive impact on those around us. We learned that our drive and determination can inspire and uplift others, fostering a supportive network that enhances our journey. By nurturing our connections and building mutual growth, we can create a ripple effect of positivity and motivation.

As we continue our journey, remember that the strength of our relationships plays a crucial role in our overall well-being and success. By fostering deeper connections and supporting one another, we can achieve more together.

Tomorrow, we'll shift our focus to the importance of balance and self-care in maintaining long-term motivation. We'll explore strategies for managing stress, prioritizing well-being, and creating a sustainable routine that supports our goals. Get ready to learn how to balance your drive with self-care to ensure lasting success and fulfillment.

Notes

> "All our dreams can come true,
> if we have the courage to pursue them."
>
> —Walt Disney

DAY 11:
CULTIVATING SELF-MOTIVATION FOR EFFECTIVE LEADERSHIP

Leadership is not limited to the corner office or the head of the table. It's a mindset, a skillset, and a way of being that can be cultivated and expressed in all areas of life. Whether you're managing a team at work, leading a group project at school, or taking initiative within your family, the principles of self-motivation can empower you to become a more effective and inspiring leader.

The Motivated Leader: Qualities and Characteristics

Motivated leaders possess a unique blend of qualities that enable them to inspire, guide, and support others[24]. They are:

- **Visionary**: They have a clear vision for the future and can communicate it in a way that inspires others to join them on the journey.
- **Passionate**: Their enthusiasm for their work or cause is contagious, igniting others' passions and fueling their motivation.
- **Empowering**: They believe in the potential of others, empowering them to take ownership, make decisions, and contribute their unique talents.
- **Resilient**: They persevere through challenges, setbacks, and failures, demonstrating unwavering determination and inspiring others to do the same.

---

24 Hanbing Xue et al., "A Meta-Analysis of Leadership and Intrinsic Motivation: Examining Relative Importance and Moderators," *Frontiers in Psychology* 13 (2022), https://doi.org/10.3389/fpsyg.2022.941161.

- *Empathetic*: They understand the needs and concerns of others and are able to connect with them on a personal level, fostering trust and rapport.
- *Accountable*: They take responsibility for their actions and decisions, hold themselves to high standards, and inspire others to do the same.
- *Adaptable*: They embrace change, remain flexible in the face of uncertainty, and are willing to learn and evolve as leaders.

Reflection:
Which of these qualities do you already possess?

_____

_____

_____

_____

Which qualities would you like to develop further?

_____

_____

_____

_____

How can you leverage your strengths to become a more effective leader?

_____

_____

_____

Leading at Work

In the workplace, motivated leaders create a culture of engagement, innovation, and high performance[25].

Actionable Steps :
- *Lead by Example*: Demonstrate the behaviors you expect from your team members.
  Example: If you expect your team to be punctual, always be on time yourself.
- *Empower Your Team*: Delegate tasks, encourage autonomy, and trust your team members.
  Example: Give your team members the authority to make decisions within their areas of expertise.
- *Communicate Effectively*: Share your vision, goals, and expectations clearly and regularly.
  Example: Hold regular team meetings to discuss progress, challenges, and upcoming projects.
- *Celebrate Success*: Recognize and reward your team's achievements, both big and small.
  Example: Publicly acknowledge individual and team accomplishments, offer bonuses or promotions, or simply say "thank you" for a job well done.
- *Foster a Positive Work Environment*: Create a workplace where people feel valued, respected, and supported.
  Example: Encourage team-building activities, provide opportunities for professional development, and create a culture of open communication.

---

25 Mohamed Alblooshi, Mohammad Shamsuzzaman, and Salah Haridy, "The Relationship between Leadership Styles and Organisational Innovation," *European Journal of Innovation Management* 24, no. 2 (2020), https://doi.org/10.1108/ejim-11-2019-0339.

Leading at School

Motivated students take charge of their learning, actively participate in class, and collaborate effectively with their peers[26].

Actionable Steps :
- ***Set Personal Learning Goals***: Clearly define what you want to achieve in each class and create a plan to reach those goals.
Example: Aim for a certain grade, master a specific skill, or complete a challenging project.
- ***Take Initiative***: Actively participate in class discussions, ask questions, and seek out additional resources to deepen your understanding.
Example: Volunteer to lead a group project, present your research to the class, or offer to help a struggling classmate.
- ***Collaborate Effectively***: Work with your peers to achieve common goals, share ideas, and learn from each other.
Example: Form study groups, participate in online forums, or collaborate on projects that require teamwork.
- ***Seek Out Feedback***: Ask your teachers for constructive feedback on your work and use it to improve.
Example: After receiving feedback on an essay, identify areas for improvement and revise your work accordingly.
- ***Celebrate Your Successes***: Acknowledge and celebrate your academic achievements, no matter how small.
Example: Reward yourself for a good grade, completing a difficult assignment, or mastering a new concept.

Leading at Home

In the home, as in any organization, motivated individuals are the cornerstone of a positive and collaborative environment. They take initiative, in-

---

26 Grassinger et al., "Interplay."

spire others, and foster a sense of shared purpose. As Rosalynn Carter wisely observed, "A leader takes people where they want to go. A great leader takes people where they don't necessarily want to go, but ought to be." This principle applies not only to presidents and CEOs but also to parents and caregivers, who must guide their families towards growth and well-being, even when faced with resistance or challenges.

Leading from home demands a unique blend of traditional leadership principles and a heightened focus on emotional intelligence. While navigating the challenges and opportunities of this environment, consider these actionable steps:

- ***Prioritize Emotional Intelligence***: Cultivate empathy and active listening skills to truly understand each family member's unique needs, motivations, and concerns.

  Example: If your teenager is struggling with online learning, instead of immediately offering solutions, take the time to listen to their frustrations and validate their feelings. This will help them feel heard and understood, making it easier to work together to find solutions. Practice reflective listening by paraphrasing what you hear to ensure understanding and show that you value their perspective. This foundation of empathy will foster open communication and pave the way for effective conflict resolution.

- ***Set Clear Expectations and Boundaries***: Establish clear and age-appropriate expectations for each family member's responsibilities and contributions to the household.

  Example: Create a chore chart that outlines daily and weekly tasks for each person or establish a shared family calendar to coordinate schedules and activities. Clearly define boundaries between work and personal life, creating dedicated spaces and times for both. This could mean setting specific work hours, turning off notifications outside of those times, or designating a quiet space for focused work. This will help maintain structure, reduce friction, and prevent burnout.

- **Lead by Example**: Model the behaviors and values you wish to see in your family. Demonstrate respect, kindness, patience, and a willingness to compromise. Show appreciation for others' efforts and acknowledge their feelings.

  Example: If you make a mistake, apologize sincerely and own up to it. If your child is struggling with a task, offer encouragement and support instead of criticism. Your actions will set the tone for the entire household and inspire others to follow suit.

- **Celebrate Achievements and Foster Collaboration**: Recognize and celebrate individual and collective achievements, both big and small. Encourage teamwork and collaboration in household chores, decision-making, and problem-solving.

  Example: Have a weekly family meeting to discuss upcoming events, share ideas, and make decisions together. Plan fun activities that involve everyone's participation, such as game nights or cooking projects. This will strengthen bonds, build trust, and create a sense of shared purpose and accomplishment.

- **Embrace Flexibility and Adaptability**: Be open to adjusting your leadership style and expectations based on the changing needs and dynamics of your family. Life is unpredictable, and so is family life. Embrace flexibility and adaptability as you navigate unexpected challenges and evolving circumstances.

  Example: If a family member is going through a difficult time, be willing to adjust schedules and expectations to provide them with the support they need. This will help you maintain a positive and supportive environment even during difficult times.

Leading with Purpose: A Lifelong Journey

Leadership is not a destination but a lifelong journey of growth and self-discovery. By cultivating self-motivation, you can become a more effective leader in all areas of your life, inspiring and empowering others to achieve their full potential. Remember, leadership is not about power or control; it's about service, influence, and making a positive impact on the world.

Notes

Carlos's Leadership Journey: Inspiring Others Through Self-Motivation

Carlos had recently been promoted to team leader at his marketing firm. While excited about the new role, he also felt immense pressure to inspire and motivate his team. He wanted to be a leader who could bring out the best in others, but he wasn't sure where to start. After a particularly challenging week, he decided to seek advice from his mentor, Maria, known for her effective leadership style.

"Maria, I'm struggling," Carlos confessed, his voice heavy with concern. "I want to be a great leader, but I feel like I'm failing to inspire my team. They seem unmotivated, and I don't know how to change that."

Maria smiled empathetically, "Leadership can be tough, Carlos, especially when you're new to it. Remember, inspiring others starts with self-motivation. How motivated are you feeling right now?"

Carlos sighed, "Honestly, I'm exhausted and a bit overwhelmed. I'm trying to keep up with my own responsibilities while leading the team, but it's a lot."

Maria nodded understandingly, "That's understandable. It's important to take care of yourself first. When you're motivated and passionate, it becomes contagious. Let's work on reigniting your own motivation and finding ways to connect with your team on a deeper level."

Reigniting Self-Motivation

Taking Maria's advice, Carlos decided to focus on his own self-motivation. He began by setting clear personal and professional goals, reminding himself why he loved his job and the impact he wanted to make. He also established a positive daily routine, incorporating exercise and mindfulness practices to boost his energy and focus.

During their next meeting, Carlos shared his progress, "Maria, I've been setting aside time each morning for a quick workout and some meditation. It's really helping me start the day with a clear mind and positive energy."

Maria smiled, "That's great to hear, Carlos. When you're feeling good and focused, it's easier to inspire your team. Now, how are you connecting with them?"

Connecting with the Team

Carlos realized that to inspire his team, he needed to understand their individual motivations and challenges. He began holding one-on-one meetings to get to know each team member better and understand their personal and professional goals.

"Hey team," Carlos announced during a meeting, "I'd like to start having regular one-on-one meetings with each of you. I want to understand your goals and see how I can support you better."

The team members responded positively, expressing their appreciation for Carlos's interest in their individual growth and aspirations.

During these meetings, Carlos actively listened to his team members, offering support and guidance. He encouraged them to pursue their passions and align their personal goals with the team's objectives.

"I want to help you achieve your goals," Carlos assured them. "If there's anything I can do to support you, please let me know. Your success is the team's success."

Leading by Example

Carlos also knew that leading by example was crucial. He made a conscious effort to demonstrate the qualities he wanted to see in his team—dedication, enthusiasm, and resilience. He arrived early, maintained a positive attitude during challenges, and celebrated even small victories.

One team member commented, "Carlos, I've noticed how you handle tough situations with such a positive attitude. It really helps boost our morale."

Carlos replied, "Thanks. I believe that maintaining a positive mindset is key to overcoming challenges. Let's focus on what we can control and keep pushing forward."

Encouraging Collaboration and Innovation

To foster a collaborative and innovative environment, Carlos encouraged open communication and idea-sharing. He implemented regular brainstorming sessions where everyone could contribute their thoughts and suggestions without fear of judgment.

"Let's have a brainstorming session every Friday," Carlos proposed. "No idea is too big or too small. I want us to think creatively and support each other's ideas."

The team embraced the idea, excited to have a dedicated space for open communication and collaboration.

Reflection

As the weeks went by, Carlos noticed a significant change in the team's dynamics. They were more engaged, motivated, and willing to take initiative. The positive energy and collaborative spirit were palpable.

Carlos's leadership journey taught him the importance of self-motivation and the power of connecting with his team on a personal level. By focusing on his own well-being, understanding his team's goals, and fostering a supportive and innovative environment, he was able to inspire others and lead effectively.

"Maria, I can't thank you enough for your guidance," Carlos expressed his gratitude during their next meeting. "Focusing on my own motivation and connecting with the team has made such a difference."

Maria smiled, "I'm glad to hear that, Carlos. Remember, effective leadership is about inspiring others through your actions and creating an environment where everyone can thrive."

Conclusion

Congratulations on completing Day 11! You've explored the qualities of a motivated leader and learned how to apply those principles in various settings. Remember, leadership is a journey, not a destination. Continue to cultivate self-motivation, empower others, and lead with integrity, and you'll make a lasting impact wherever you go.

Tomorrow, we'll shift gears and delve into the art of decluttering and organizing your physical space to create an environment that nurtures your well-being and fuels your motivation. As Peter Walsh wisely said, "Clutter is not just the stuff on your floor—it's anything that stands between you and the life you want to be living." By clearing out physical clutter, we create space for mental clarity, focus, and creativity, ultimately enhancing our productivity and overall well-being.

Notes

PART V:
M – MAP OUT YOUR PATH

"The only person you are destined to become
is the person you decide to be."

—Ralph Waldo Emerson

DAY 12:
CULTIVATING YOUR OASIS

In the previous chapter, we delved into the profound impact of self-motivation on our relationships, discovering that our drive and determination can ripple outward, enriching our connections and fostering mutual growth. We learned how to build a supportive social environment through effective communication, empathy, and shared goals.

Today, we'll shift gears to explore the crucial balance between our drive and self-care. While our ambition propels us forward, it's equally important to prioritize our well-being to ensure long-term success. Think of it like a high-performance car—it needs regular maintenance and fuel to operate at its best. Similarly, your body and mind require care and attention to maintain optimal performance.

Imagine trying to focus on a complex task in a chaotic, noisy room filled with distractions. It's like trying to swim upstream against a raging current. Now picture yourself in a serene, organized space with soft lighting, calming music, and everything you need within reach. In this peaceful environment, your mind can freely flow, your creativity can blossom, and your motivation can soar.

Just as a well-designed space can nurture your focus and creativity, a balanced approach to self-care can fuel your motivation and drive. In this chapter, we'll explore the art of creating a harmonious balance between ambition and well-being. We'll delve into strategies for managing stress, prioritizing self-care, and designing a sustainable routine that supports your goals. By integrating self-care into your daily life, you'll not only avoid burnout but also enhance your overall productivity and well-being.

Creating Your Personal Haven

Declutter and Organize: A cluttered space is a cluttered mind. Take some time to declutter your workspace, home, or any other environment where you spend significant time. Organize your belongings, create designated spaces for different activities, and get rid of anything that doesn't serve a purpose or bring you joy. What specific steps will you take to declutter and organize your space to create a more focused and productive environment?

_____

_____

_____

_____

Personalize Your Space: Surround yourself with items that inspire and motivate you. This could include photos of loved ones, motivational quotes, artwork, plants, or anything else that sparks joy and creativity. What specific items would you like to incorporate into your surroundings to create a more inspiring and motivating atmosphere? How will you arrange or display them to maximize their impact on your daily life?

_____

_____

_____

_____

Optimize Lighting: Natural light is ideal for boosting mood and energy levels, so try to position your workspace near a window. If natural light isn't available, use full-spectrum light bulbs that mimic natural sunlight. Avoid harsh fluorescent lighting, which can be draining. What steps can you take to maximize natural light in your workspace or living areas? If natural light is limited, what alternative lighting options can you explore to create a more energizing and uplifting environment?

_____

_____

_____

_____

Incorporate Calming Colors: Colors have a powerful impact on our emotions and energy levels. Opt for calming colors like blues, greens, and neutrals in your workspace or relaxation areas. Avoid overly stimulating colors like bright reds and oranges, which can be distracting. What colors do you find calming and conducive to focus? How can you incorporate these colors into your workspace or relaxation areas to promote a more serene and productive environment?

_____

_____

_____

_____

Add Plants and Nature: Bringing nature indoors can have a profound impact on our well-being. Plants not only purify the air but also reduce stress, boost creativity, and improve focus. Consider adding a few houseplants to your space or creating a small indoor garden. What specific types of houseplants or greenery would you like to incorporate into your space? How can you best arrange or care for them to maximize their positive impact on your well-being and create a more inviting environment?

___

Create a Designated Workspace: If possible, designate a specific area for work or creative projects. This will help you establish a routine and minimize distractions. Make sure your workspace is comfortable, well-lit, and equipped with everything you need to be productive. What steps can you take to create a dedicated workspace that is conducive to focus and productivity? How will you ensure it is equipped with the necessary tools and resources to support your work or creative projects?

___

Control Noise and Temperature: Noise and temperature can significantly impact our focus and productivity. If possible, create a quiet workspace or use noise-canceling headphones. Keep the temperature at a comfortable level, as extreme temperatures can be distracting and uncomfortable. What steps can you take to reduce noise levels in your workspace, such as using noise-canceling headphones or relocating to a quieter area? How can you ensure that the temperature in your workspace is consistently comfortable and conducive to focus?

___

___

___

___

Incorporate Motivational Reminders: Place motivational quotes, images, or objects in your line of sight. These visual cues can serve as powerful reminders of your goals and aspirations, inspiring you to stay on track. What motivational quotes, images, or objects resonate with you the most? Where would you place them in your environment to ensure they are visible and serve as daily reminders of your goals and aspirations?

___

___

___

___

Create a Vision Board: A vision board is a collage of images, words, and quotes that represent your goals and dreams. It's a powerful visualization tool that can help you stay motivated and focused on what you want to achieve. What specific images, words, or quotes would you include on your vision board to represent your goals and dreams? Where would you place this vision board to ensure it serves as a daily reminder of your aspirations?

___

Your environment is a reflection of your inner world. By creating a space that is organized, inspiring, and conducive to your goals, you're sending a powerful message to your subconscious mind that you're committed to success. So, take the time to curate your environment and watch your motivation flourish.

Jake's Home Office Transformation: Creating a Space for Success

Jake had been working from home for over a year, and his makeshift workspace was taking a toll on his productivity. His desk was cluttered, his chair was uncomfortable, and the overall environment was far from inspiring. He knew he needed a change but felt overwhelmed by the task. One day, after a particularly unproductive week, he decided to seek advice from his friend, Emma, an interior designer known for creating functional and inspiring home offices.

"Emma, I'm at my wit's end," Jake vented, frustration evident in his voice. "My home office is a disaster, and it's seriously affecting my work. I need help."

Emma smiled reassuringly, "I'm glad you reached out, Jake. A well-designed workspace can make a huge difference. Let's take a look at your setup and see what we can do."

Assessing the Current Setup

Emma visited Jake's home to assess his current workspace. The desk was piled high with papers, cables were tangled everywhere, and the lighting was dim. It was clear that Jake's office needed a complete overhaul.

"Alright, first things first," Emma declared, looking around. "We need to declutter and organize. A cluttered space leads to a cluttered mind. Let's start by sorting through these papers and getting rid of anything you don't need."

Jake nodded in agreement, "Sounds good. I've been meaning to do that for a while."

Decluttering and Organizing

Jake and Emma spent the next few hours sorting through the clutter. They categorized papers, organized supplies, and discarded unnecessary items. Once the desk was clear, Emma suggested adding some storage solutions to keep things tidy.

"Now that we've decluttered, let's add some storage," Emma proposed. "Shelves, drawers, and baskets will help keep everything in its place. Also, let's organize your cables with some cable management tools."

Jake was already feeling more optimistic, "I never realized how much clutter was affecting me. This already feels better."

Optimizing the Layout

With the clutter cleared, Emma and Jake focused on optimizing the layout of the room. They rearranged the furniture to create a more open and functional space. Emma suggested positioning Jake's desk near the window to take advantage of natural light.

"Natural light is great for boosting mood and productivity," Emma explained. "Let's move your desk over here by the window."

Jake agreed, "Good idea. I love the view from here, too. It'll be nice to look outside while I work."

Adding Personal Touches

Emma then recommended adding some personal touches to make the space more inviting and inspiring. They picked out some artwork, a few plants, and a comfortable chair.

"Adding personal touches makes the space feel more like your own," Emma advised. "What kind of artwork do you like? And let's get a plant or two; they can really brighten up the space."

Jake's face lit up, "I have a few photos from my travels that I'd love to hang up. And I've always wanted a couple of plants in here."

Final Touches

After rearranging and decorating, they added some final touches to enhance the functionality of the workspace. Emma suggested a whiteboard for jotting down ideas and a cozy rug to make the space more comfortable.

"A whiteboard is great for brainstorming and keeping track of your to-do list," Emma pointed out. "And this rug will add some warmth to the room."

Jake was thrilled with the results, "This is amazing, Emma. The space feels completely different now. I can't wait to start working here."

Jake's home office transformation was more than just a physical makeover; it was a catalyst for a profound shift in his mindset and productivity. The newly organized and personalized space fostered a sense of calm and focus, igniting a renewed energy within him.

"Emma," Jake said with genuine gratitude, "I can't thank you enough. This space is exactly what I needed. I already feel more motivated and engaged with my work."

Emma beamed, "I'm so happy to hear that, Jake. Remember, a well-designed workspace can have a significant impact on your well-being and performance. Keep it tidy, and don't hesitate to make adjustments as your needs evolve."

Jake's experience exemplifies the transformative power of creating a conducive work environment. By decluttering, organizing, and infusing his personality into the space, he turned his home office into a sanctuary for productivity and success. His journey serves as a reminder that our surroundings play a crucial role in shaping our mindset and, ultimately, our achievements.

As you work on creating your own oasis, remember that the environment you work in can significantly impact your productivity and well-being. Take the time to assess your current setup, make necessary changes, and create a space that inspires you to do your best work.

Conclusion

Today, we focused on the essential balance between drive and self-care. We explored how integrating self-care into our daily routines can help us manage stress, maintain motivation, and achieve long-term success. By prioritizing our well-being and creating sustainable habits, we ensure that our drive remains strong and that we avoid burnout. We learned practical strategies to balance our ambitions with the care our bodies and minds need to thrive.

As you continue your journey, remember that self-care is not a luxury but a necessity. It is the foundation upon which sustainable success is built. By taking care of yourself, you ensure that you have the energy and resilience needed to pursue your goals with passion and dedication.

Tomorrow, we'll delve into the power of reflection and celebration in maintaining motivation. We'll explore how looking back on our achievements and celebrating our progress can fuel our drive and keep us focused on our journey. Get ready to learn why recognizing your successes is important and how it can inspire you to keep moving forward with renewed energy and enthusiasm.

"These virtues are formed in man by his doing the actions . . . we are what we repeatedly do. Excellence, then, is not an act but a habit."

—Aristotle[27]

---

27 Aristotle, as paraphrased by Will Durant in "The Story of Philosophy."

DAY 13:
HARNESSING THE POWER OF HABIT FOR LASTING MOTIVATION

In the previous chapter, we focused on the importance of cultivating your personal oasis—a dedicated space that nurtures your well-being and fuels your motivation. We explored how our environment can significantly impact our productivity, creativity, and overall sense of peace. By decluttering, organizing, and personalizing your space, you learned to create a sanctuary that supports your journey towards your dreams.

Today, we'll delve into the power of habit and how it can be harnessed to sustain lasting motivation. Habits are the building blocks of our daily routines, shaping our actions and ultimately determining our success. By understanding the science behind habit formation and learning how to develop positive habits, you can create a strong foundation for achieving your goals.

Consider your habits to be grooves etched into a well-worn path. The more you walk that path, the deeper the grooves become, and the easier it is to continue walking it. Similarly, the more you repeat a behavior, the more ingrained it becomes, and the less effort it takes to maintain it. By consciously choosing the habits you want to cultivate, you can steer your life in the direction of your dreams.

In this chapter, we'll explore strategies for breaking free from old, unproductive patterns and establishing new, empowering habits that align with your aspirations. We'll uncover the secrets to making lasting changes and discover how the transformative power of habit can keep your motivation alive and propel you toward your goals.

The Science of Habit Formation

Imagine a snowball rolling down a hill. At first, it's small and slow, but as it gathers momentum, it grows larger and faster, becoming an unstoppable force. Our habits work in a similar way. They start as small, seemingly insignificant actions, but over time, they can compound into significant results, shaping our lives and driving our success.

Habits are deeply ingrained patterns of behavior that are triggered by specific cues and reinforced by rewards[28]. They operate on a loop consisting of three elements:

1. ***Cue***: A trigger that prompts habitual behavior. This could be a time of day, a location, an emotional state, or a preceding event.
2. ***Routine***: The habitual behavior itself, which can be physical, mental, or emotional.
3. ***Reward:*** The positive outcome or feeling associated with the behavior, which reinforces the habit and makes it more likely to be repeated.

Understanding this loop is key to creating and breaking habits. By identifying the cues that trigger your desired behavior, establishing a consistent routine, and rewarding yourself for your efforts, you can create powerful habits that support your goals and fuel your motivation.

Breaking the Chains: Michael's Journey to Freedom from Smoking

The salty sea breeze carried the faint scent of sunscreen and fried seafood as Michael leaned against the weathered wooden railing of the pier, cigarette smoke curling around his fingers. He gazed out at the endless expanse of blue, a familiar ache in his chest. This was his ritual, his escape, a moment of solitude amidst the chaos of life. But today, something felt different. The cigarette tasted bitter; the smoke was harsh in his lungs. It was a reminder of the doctor's words, the warning etched on the pack, the nagging voice in his head that echoed his wife's plea—"Please quit, Michael."

---

28 Carden and Wood, "Habit Formation."

He knew he should quit. He understood the health risks, the financial burden, and the strain on his relationships. Yet, every attempt ended in frustration. He'd white-knuckle through a few days, maybe a week, before the cravings became an insatiable beast. Stress at work, a fight with his wife, a long drive—any triggering event was enough to send him scrambling for a smoke.

Michael didn't realize that his smoking habit was more than just a physical addiction to nicotine. It was deeply ingrained in his daily routines—a complex web of triggers and rewards that reinforced the behavior. The morning cup of coffee, the after-dinner ritual, and the break at work—each of these moments had become inextricably linked to lighting up. The nicotine rush, the temporary relief from stress, the feeling of belonging with other smokers – these rewards further cemented the habit.

One evening, as he watched his young daughter cough from secondhand smoke, a wave of guilt washed over him. He resolved to try again, but this time armed with a new understanding. He started by identifying his triggers—the times and places where he was most likely to crave a cigarette. He then found alternative activities to replace the act of smoking. When he felt stressed, he went for a walk on the beach instead of reaching for a cigarette. After dinner, he played a game with his daughter instead of indulging in his usual smoke.

Slowly but surely, the cravings lessened, and the triggers lost their power. He discovered new joys in the activities that replaced smoking. He noticed an improved taste of food, increased energy, and clarity of mind. He felt healthier, happier, and more connected to his family.

One morning, as he stood on the pier, the salty breeze filling his lungs with fresh air, he realized that he had finally broken free from the chains of his habit. The ocean stretched out before him, a symbol of infinite possibilities and a reminder that change, like the tides, is a constant force. He smiled, knowing that he had taken the first step towards a healthier, smoke-free future.

Harnessing the Power of Habit for Motivation

Habits are the invisible architecture of our daily lives. They can be both a blessing and a curse, shaping our actions and outcomes in profound ways. While bad habits can sabotage our efforts and hold us back, good habits, as Octavia Butler wisely stated, "are more dependable. Habit will sustain you whether you're inspired or not. Habit is persistence in practice." By intentionally creating and cultivating positive habits, we can harness this power to boost our motivation, enhance our productivity, and create lasting change in our lives.

Here are some strategies for harnessing the power of habit for motivation:

- ***Start Small***: Don't try to make drastic changes. Start with small, manageable changes that you can easily incorporate into your daily routine. For example, instead of trying to go to the gym for an hour every day, start with a 15-minute walk. What one small action will you commit to today to start building a positive habit?

_____

_____

_____

_____

- ***Focus on One Habit at a Time***: Instead of trying to change everything at once, focus on making incremental changes to a few key habits. This approach can help you avoid feeling overwhelmed and increase your chances of long-term success. Which bad habit will you commit to changing now?

_____

- ***Identify Your Cues***: What triggers your desired behavior? Every habit, good or bad, is usually triggered by specific cues in our environment or internal states. Is it a specific time of day, a location, or an emotional state? For instance, feeling stressed might trigger emotional eating, or seeing your phone might lead to mindless scrolling. To change a bad habit, you need to first identify what triggers it. Pay close attention to the situations, emotions, or thoughts that precede your habit. What patterns do you notice? Once you identify your cues, you can create an environment that supports your habit. If certain people or places trigger your habit, try to avoid them or create a plan for how you'll respond differently in those situations. What triggers will you start to work on changing?

- ***Create a Consistent Routine***: Establish a clear and consistent routine for your desired behavior. This will make it easier to stick to your habit and feel more automatic. What habits will you start to make routine?

- ***Reward Yourself***: Celebrate your successes, no matter how small they may seem. Rewards reinforce positive behavior and make it more likely that you'll continue the habit. How will you celebrate your success?

- ***Track Your Progress***: Keeping track of your progress can help you stay motivated and identify areas where you need to improve. Use a journal, app, or calendar to track your habit streak and celebrate your milestones. Commit to journaling, capturing your thoughts and progress.
- ***Be Patient and Persistent***: Habit formation takes time and effort. Don't get discouraged if you slip up or have setbacks. Just get back on track and keep going. Remember, consistency is key. As William Makepeace Thackeray said, "Successful people aren't born that way. They become successful by establishing the habit of doing things unsuccessful people don't like to do."

By harnessing the power of habit, you can create a positive feedback loop that fuels your motivation and propels you toward your goals. As you cultivate empowering habits, you'll find yourself making progress, feeling more confident, and achieving success in all areas of your life.

In the next chapter, we'll explore another powerful tool for enhancing motivation and well-being: mindfulness.

Conclusion

As we wrap up our discussion on harnessing the power of habit, remember that consistent actions lead to lasting change. By cultivating habits that support your goals, you can create a routine that propels you forward with steady, sustainable progress. Each small, positive habit you establish is a step towards achieving your dreams.

Tomorrow, we will delve into the role of self-motivation as a catalyst for lifelong learning and growth. We'll explore how a commitment to continuous learning can expand your horizons, enhance your skills, and keep your motivation vibrant. Get ready to embrace a mindset of curiosity and discovery as we unlock the transformative power of lifelong learning.

Notes

PART VI:

S - SUSTAIN MOMENTUM THROUGH SETBACKS

"Our greatest weakness lies in giving up. The most certain way to succeed is always to try just one more time."

—Thomas A. Edison

DAY 14:
SELF-MOTIVATION AS THE CATALYST

On Day 13, we explored the powerful concept of habit formation and how establishing positive habits can significantly enhance our motivation and productivity. We explored the science behind habit formation, emphasizing the importance of consistency and small, manageable changes. By harnessing the power of habit, we learned how to build a strong foundation for long-term success and personal growth.

Today, we'll shift our focus to self-motivation as a catalyst for lifelong learning and continuous improvement. Lifelong learning is not just about acquiring new knowledge or skills; it's about maintaining a curious and open mindset that allows us to adapt and thrive in an ever-changing world. By integrating self-motivation into our learning journey, we can unlock new opportunities, enhance our personal and professional lives, and achieve a deeper sense of fulfillment.

Embracing Lifelong Learning

Your journey of self-motivation doesn't end with achieving specific goals; it's a lifelong process of learning, growth, and transformation. By harnessing the power of self-motivation, you can unlock your full potential, expand your horizons, and create a life that is both fulfilling and meaningful.

Cultivate a Curiosity Mindset: Approach life with a sense of wonder and a thirst for knowledge. Ask questions, seek out new experiences, and challenge your assumptions. Embrace the unknown, and view learning as an exciting adventure.

Reflection: What questions have you been curious about lately? What new topics or skills would you like to explore?

_____

_____

_____

_____

Set Learning Goals: Identify areas where you want to grow and develop. Whether it's learning a new language, mastering a new skill, or deepening your understanding of a particular subject, setting clear learning goals can provide focus and direction.

Action Step: Write down three specific learning goals you want to achieve in the next six months.

_____

_____

_____

_____

Explore Diverse Learning Opportunities: Don't limit yourself to traditional methods of learning. Take advantage of the wealth of resources available today, from online courses and workshops to books, podcasts, and documentaries.

Brainstorm: List three unconventional ways you could learn something new (e.g., attending a workshop, joining a discussion group, volunteering for a project).

_____

_____

_____

_____

Embrace Challenges: Confront difficult tasks and subjects head-on; they are opportunities for learning and development. Stepping outside your comfort zone is where the real growth happens. Challenges should be seen as opportunities to learn, expand your skills, and build resilience.

Reflection: What is one challenging skill or subject you've been avoiding? How can you approach it with a growth mindset?

_____

_____

_____

_____

Reflect on Your Learning: Take time to reflect on what you've learned, how you've grown, and what you can do differently in the future. Journaling, meditation, or simply taking a quiet walk can help you process your experiences and integrate new knowledge.

Action Step: Start a learning journal to document your progress, insights, and reflections on your learning journey.

___

Share Your Knowledge: Teaching others is a powerful way to solidify your own understanding and contribute to the growth of others. Share your insights, experiences, and expertise with others through writing, speaking, mentoring, or volunteering.

Brainstorm: How can you share your knowledge and expertise with others? (e.g., mentoring, writing a blog post, teaching a class)

___

Create a Supportive Learning Environment: Surround yourself with people who inspire and challenge you to grow. Join a book club, participate in online forums, or find a mentor who can guide you on your learning journey.

Action Step: Join a club, group, or online community where you can connect with others who share your interests and learn from each other.

_____

_____

_____

_____

Expanding Your Horizons

Self-motivation can also fuel your desire to explore new horizons and expand your experience. Here are some ways to broaden your perspective and enrich your life:

Travel: Experiencing different cultures, meeting new people, and exploring new places can open your mind, broaden your perspective, and spark new ideas.

Reflection: If you could travel anywhere in the world, where would you go and why?

_____

_____

_____

_____

Engage in Creative Pursuits: Express yourself through art, music, writing, or other creative outlets. Creativity can be a source of joy, inspiration, and personal growth.

Action Step: Choose one creative activity you've always wanted to try and commit to practicing it for at least 30 minutes a day for a week.

___

Connect with Nature: Spending time in nature can improve mood, reduce stress, and boost creativity. Take a hike, go for a swim, or simply sit in a park and observe the natural world.

Action Step: Plan a nature outing for this week, whether it's a hike, a walk in the park, or simply sitting under a tree.

___

Volunteer Your Time: Helping others can give you a sense of purpose and fulfillment. It can also expose you to new perspectives and challenges, fostering personal growth.

Research: Find three volunteer opportunities in your community that align with your interests and values.

Challenge Your Assumptions: Question your beliefs and assumptions about the world. Be open to new ideas and perspectives, even if they challenge your comfort zone.

Reflection: What is one belief or assumption you hold that you could challenge or question?

The Transformative Power of Self-Motivation

By embracing lifelong learning and expanding your horizons, you'll not only enhance your knowledge and skills but also transform yourself into a more well-rounded, adaptable, and resilient individual. Self-motivation is the fuel that propels you on this journey of growth and transformation, empowering you to create a life that is rich in meaning, purpose, and joy.

As you continue your journey of self-motivation, remember that personal growth is an ongoing process. There's always something new to learn, explore, and discover. Embrace the challenges, celebrate your successes, and never stop learning. Your potential is limitless.

Notes

Raj's Ironman Training: Staying Motivated for the Long Haul

Raj had always been an avid athlete, but attempting an IRONMAN triathlon was a new level of challenge. The idea of completing a 2.4-mile swim, a 112-mile bike ride, and a 26.2-mile run all in one day seemed daunting. However, it was a challenge that he was determined to conquer. With an IRONMAN event scheduled in six months, he began his training with enthusiasm. As the weeks passed, Raj found it increasingly difficult to stay motivated. After a particularly grueling training session, he reached out to his friend, Jake, an experienced Ironman competitor, for advice.

"Jake, I don't know how you do it," Raj said, panting heavily. "I'm halfway through my training plan, and I'm already feeling burnt out. It's so hard to stay motivated."

Jake smiled understandingly, "I've been there, Raj. Ironman training is as much a mental challenge as it is a physical one. What's been the hardest part for you?"

Raj explained, "Honestly, it's the monotony. Training for three different disciplines, the long hours—it's starting to feel like a grind. I need something to keep me going."

Jake suggested, "Mixing things up and finding new sources of motivation can make a big difference. Have you tried joining a training group or setting smaller goals along the way?"

Finding New Motivation

Taking Jake's advice, Raj decided to join a local triathlon training group. The camaraderie and support of fellow athletes injected new energy into his training. He also set smaller, incremental goals to keep himself motivated.

"Jake, I joined a triathlon group!" Raj exclaimed enthusiastically during their next conversation. "It's great to have people to train with and share the journey. We even do group swims and bike rides on weekends."

"That's awesome, Raj," Jake replied. "Training with others can really boost your motivation. And setting smaller goals?"

Raj explained, "I'm aiming for personal bests in each discipline and rewarding myself when I hit them. It's helping to break up the long-term goal into more manageable chunks."

Overcoming Setbacks

Despite the renewed motivation, Raj faced setbacks. A minor injury forced him to take a break from training, which frustrated him and threatened to derail his progress. He called Jake to get some encouragement.

"Jake, I pulled a muscle and have to take a break," Raj said, frustration evident in his voice. "I'm worried this will set me back too much."

Jake reassured him, "Injuries are part of the process, Raj. It's important to listen to your body and give it time to heal. Focus on what you can do—maybe some strength exercises or yoga that won't strain the injury."

Raj felt a bit better, "I guess you're right. I'll use this time to work on my core and flexibility. Thanks for the perspective."

Staying Mentally Strong

As Raj continued his training, he realized the importance of mental resilience. Long training sessions, particularly the back-to-back bike rides and runs, were especially challenging, testing his mental stamina as much as his physical endurance. He developed strategies to stay focused and positive.

"Jake, those long bike rides followed by runs are killer," Raj admitted. "How do you keep your mind from wandering and wanting to quit?"

Jake shared his experience, "It's all about finding your flow and staying mentally engaged. I like to break the training into segments and focus on each one. Sometimes, I listen to motivational podcasts or music to keep my mind occupied."

Raj nodded, "I'll try that. Maybe breaking it down into smaller parts will help. And I love the idea of listening to something engaging."

Race Day

The day of the IRONMAN finally arrived. Raj felt a mix of excitement and nerves. He remembered all the advice and encouragement Jake had given him and felt ready to tackle the challenge.

"Here we go," Raj thought to himself at the starting line. "One step at a time, just like Jake said."

As Raj swam, biked, and ran, he broke the race into smaller segments, focusing on reaching each milestone. He drew strength from the crowd's energy and his fellow competitors. When the race got tough, he reminded himself of the progress he had made and the setbacks he had overcome.

"You've got this," he repeated to himself. "Just keep moving forward."

Crossing the finish line was an exhilarating moment. Raj felt a surge of pride and accomplishment, knowing he had stayed motivated and persevered through the challenges.

Jake hugged Raj at the finish line, "You did it, Raj! How do you feel?"

Raj, breathless but elated, replied, "I feel amazing! It was tough, but all the hard work paid off. Thanks for all your support, Jake."

Raj's Ironman journey taught him the importance of maintaining motivation through camaraderie, setting smaller goals, and staying mentally strong. He realized that perseverance and a positive mindset were key to achieving his long-term goal.

"Jake, I couldn't have done it without your advice and support," Raj expressed his gratitude. "This has been an incredible journey."

Jake smiled, "You did the work, Raj. Remember, it's not just about the race, but the journey and growth along the way."

Conclusion

Today, we've explored the transformative power of self-motivation as a catalyst for lifelong learning. We've seen how maintaining a curious and open mindset can help us adapt to new challenges and continuously improve ourselves. By embracing lifelong learning, we can unlock new opportunities, enhance our personal and professional lives, and achieve a deeper sense of fulfillment.

As we continue our journey, remember that the path to success is a continuous process of learning and growth. Keep nurturing your curiosity, seeking out new knowledge, and staying motivated to improve every day.

Tomorrow, we will delve into the importance of embracing life's challenges and how to turn them into opportunities for growth. We'll explore strategies for overcoming obstacles and developing resilience, which are essential for maintaining motivation and achieving our long-term goals. Get ready to face your challenges head-on and transform them into stepping-stones towards success.

Notes

"Our greatest glory is not in never falling,
but in rising every time we fall."

—Confucius

DAY 15:
EMBRACING LIFE'S CHALLENGES

In the previous chapter, we explored the transformative power of self-motivation as a catalyst for lifelong learning and personal growth. We delved into the concept of embracing challenges as opportunities, highlighting how continuous learning can expand our horizons and fuel our motivation. Raj's inspiring journey of preparing for an Ironman competition illustrated the importance of resilience, mental strength, and the pursuit of new motivations.

Today, we'll focus on the importance of embracing life's challenges. Challenges and setbacks are inevitable parts of life, but how we respond to them can significantly impact our growth and success. By learning to navigate life's challenges effectively, we can maintain our motivation, achieve our goals, and lead a fulfilling life. We'll explore strategies for overcoming fears, finding balance amidst multiple passions, and creating routines that allow us to thrive despite obstacles. Remember, as Helen Keller wisely said, "Character cannot be developed in ease and quiet. Only through experience of trial and suffering can the soul be strengthened, ambition inspired, and success achieved."

Life's Journey

In life's journey, you will inevitably encounter obstacles, setbacks, and moments of doubt. Some obstacles may be beyond your control, while others are created within your mind. Amidst these challenges, self-motivation is the force that will propel you forward. It's the fire within that fuels your determination, resilience, and unwavering belief in your abilities.

Dr. Wayne Dyer's words, "Don't die with your music still inside of you[29]," are a powerful call to action. Your unique contributions are meant to be shared, to uplift, and to connect with others. To unleash your true potential, it's crucial to understand what holds you back.

What specific fears and anxieties keep you from stepping into your own spotlight? Are you afraid of the unknown, the consequences of your actions, or the possibility of failure? These are common fears that can feel paralyzing. However, by confronting your fears directly, you open the door to liberation. Embracing uncertainty reveals your resilience, adaptability, and the immense possibilities that lie ahead. Remember, the music inside you is waiting to be heard. It's time to let it play.

The Power of Writing Down Your Fears

There's immense power in acknowledging your fears and anxieties. By putting pen to paper, you demystify them, bringing them into the light where they can be examined and overcome. Imagine releasing your fears like leaves carried away by the wind. Visualize them leaving your mind, freeing you from their grip. This act of externalizing anxieties can be incredibly empowering.

Take a moment for introspection. What anxieties or doubts are holding you back? Are you struggling with:

- Perfectionism: The relentless pursuit of flawlessness?
- Imposter Syndrome: The nagging feeling of being a fraud?
- Fear of Rejection: The dread of criticism or disapproval?
- Fear of Vulnerability: The hesitation to show your true self?

Fear is a natural human emotion, but it doesn't have to control your life. By identifying and naming your fears, you empower yourself to choose a different path—one of clarity, courage, and growth.

---

29 Dyer, Serena J. J. and Wayne W. Dyer, *Don't Die with Your Music Still in You: My Experience Growing Up with Spiritual Parents*, first edition. (n.p.: Hay House, 2014).

Life's unpredictable nature and our innate resistance to change often leave us standing at a crossroads. One path leads to the graveyard of unfulfilled dreams, paved with fear and inaction. The other path, less traveled, leads to a life of limitless possibilities, where your music can finally be heard. The choice is ours.

Let's choose to embrace the unknown, confront our fears head-on, and unleash the creative potential that lies dormant within us. Let's transform our doubts into steppingstones, our imperfections into unique marks of authenticity, and our vulnerabilities into sources of strength.

By internalizing the empowering perspectives shared in this chapter and taking bold action, we can overcome our fears and step into the brilliance that awaits us. Remember, your voice is important, and the world is eager to hear your unique melody.

As Dale Carnegie wisely said, "Inaction breeds doubt and fear. Action breeds confidence and courage. If you want to conquer fear, do not sit at home and think about it. Go out and get busy." By taking action despite your fears, you'll not only overcome them but also create space for personal fulfillment.

Write down your fears. As you confront them, they will begin to lose their power. Remember, these anxieties are not unique to you. Even the most accomplished individuals have grappled with these same demons.

My Fears and Anxieties:

_____

_____

_____

_____

Congratulations! You've taken the first step toward conquering your fears.

Reframing Your Thoughts and Fears

By conquering your fears, you unlock a universe of possibilities. Once liberated from self-doubt, your work can transcend obscurity, becoming a radiant beacon that guides and illuminates the lives of others.

To reframe your fear and transform it into a catalyst for growth, consider these empowering perspectives:

- ***Embrace imperfection***: No work is perfect. Imperfections often make art more interesting and relatable.
- ***Focus on the process***: Shift your focus from the fear of judgment to the joy of creating and sharing.
- Seek support: Surround yourself with a supportive community of fellow creatives who can offer encouragement and feedback.
- ***Start small***: Begin by sharing your work with a trusted circle of friends or family before venturing out to a wider audience.
- ***Celebrate courage***: Acknowledge and celebrate the courage it takes to put yourself out there, regardless of the outcome.

By internalizing these perspectives and taking action, you'll overcome your fears and unleash the full potential of your creativity. Remember: Your voice matters, and the world is waiting to hear it.

This journey from fear to freedom opens a world of possibilities where your dreams can flourish. Perhaps you've always yearned to start a business, write a book, travel the world, or simply live a more authentic life. Whatever those aspirations may be, they are now within your reach.

It's time to shift your focus from limitations to inspiration. Discover the passions that have been lying dormant, waiting for you to awaken them. Let's delve into the exhilarating process of nurturing your dreams now that you are empowered to embrace them fully.

Sophia's Dual Passions: Balancing Career and Hobbies

Sophia was a dedicated software engineer who loved her job, but she also had a deep passion for painting. For years, she struggled to find time for her art while keeping up with her demanding career. She often felt guilty for not dedicating enough time to her hobbies and overwhelmed by her workload. One day, after another long week at the office, she decided to seek advice from her friend, Rachel, who had successfully balanced her career as a lawyer with her love for gardening.

"Rachel, I'm really struggling," Sophia confessed, her voice heavy with frustration. "I love my job, but I also miss painting. I feel like there's never enough time to do both, and I'm constantly torn between work and my passion."

Rachel nodded understandingly, "I understand, Sophia. It's challenging to balance a demanding career with personal interests. But it's definitely possible. Have you tried scheduling dedicated time for your hobbies?"

Sophia sighed, "I've tried, but work always seems to take over. By the time I get home, I'm too exhausted to pick up a paintbrush."

Rachel suggested, "Maybe it's about finding a routine that works for you. Let's brainstorm some ideas to help you make time for both."

Creating a Balanced Routine

With Rachel's help, Sophia decided to create a more structured routine. She blocked out specific times in her calendar for painting and made a commitment to stick to those times as much as possible. She also looked for ways to make her work schedule more efficient, such as delegating tasks when possible and setting realistic deadlines.

"Rachel, I've started blocking out time in my calendar for painting," Sophia reported during their next chat. "I'm trying to treat it like any other important meeting or task."

"That's a great start, Sophia," Rachel replied. "Also, look for ways to streamline your work tasks. Maybe you can set boundaries, like not checking emails after a certain time, to give yourself more mental space for your art."

Sophia agreed, "I'll definitely try that. Setting boundaries sounds like a good idea."

Setting Boundaries and Prioritizing
Sophia began setting clear boundaries with her work. She communicated with her team about her availability and made sure to finish her work within the designated hours. This allowed her to have evenings free for painting. She also prioritized her tasks, focusing on the most important ones first to avoid last-minute rushes and late nights at the office.

"Hey team," Sophia announced during a meeting, "I've decided to set some boundaries to improve my work-life balance. I'll be focusing on finishing tasks during work hours and won't be checking emails after 7 PM. I appreciate your understanding."

Her colleagues were supportive, acknowledging the importance of work-life balance and respecting her decision.

Finding Joy in the Process
As Sophia started to dedicate more time to painting, she rediscovered the joy it brought her. She found that having a creative outlet helped her relax and recharge, which in turn made her more productive and focused at work.

"Rachel, painting again feels amazing," Sophia exclaimed during their next conversation. "It's like I've found a part of myself that I'd forgotten about. I'm more relaxed and even more productive at work."

Rachel smiled, "That's wonderful, Sophia. It's amazing how having a creative outlet can positively impact other areas of your life. Keep nurturing both your career and your passion."

Integrating Passions into Daily Life

Sophia also looked for small ways to integrate her love for art into her daily life. She began carrying a sketchbook and used her lunch breaks to do quick sketches or visit art galleries. This helped her stay connected to her passion, even on the busiest days.

"Rachel, I've started carrying a sketchbook with me," Sophia shared. "I use my lunch breaks to do quick sketches or visit art galleries. It keeps me connected to my art, even on hectic days."

Rachel nodded approvingly, "That's a brilliant idea, Sophia. It's all about finding those little moments to do what you love. It doesn't always have to be a big, dedicated time block."

Over time, Sophia found a balance between her career and her passion for painting. She realized that setting boundaries, prioritizing her tasks, and finding joy in the process were key to maintaining a fulfilling work-life balance.

"Rachel, I can't thank you enough for your advice," Sophia expressed her gratitude. "I've found a way to balance my career and my painting, and it's made a huge difference in my life."

Rachel smiled, "I'm so happy to hear that, Sophia. Remember, it's all about making time for what you love and finding a routine that works for you."

Conclusion

Today, we delved into the power of embracing life's challenges. We learned that obstacles are not just barriers but opportunities for growth and learning. By facing our fears, balancing our passions, and setting priorities, we can create a balanced and fulfilling routine that supports our goals. Sophia's journey of balancing her career and hobbies demonstrated the importance of setting boundaries, prioritizing joy in the process, and integrating passions into daily life.

As we move forward, remember that challenges are not roadblocks but steppingstones towards a more resilient and fulfilled self. Embrace each challenge with a growth mindset, and let it propel you towards your dreams.

Tomorrow, we will explore the profound impact of gratitude and positive affirmations on our motivation and overall well-being. We will learn how expressing gratitude and practicing positive self-talk can transform our mindset, enhance our resilience, and sustain our momentum. Get ready to unlock the power of gratitude and affirmations as we continue our journey towards achieving our dreams.

Notes

"When you dance, your purpose is not to get to a certain place on the floor. It's to enjoy each step along the way."

—Dr. Dwayne Dyer

DAY 16:
SHOWING GRATITUDE AND POSITIVE AFFIRMATIONS

On Day 15, we explored the power of embracing life's challenges. We delved into how obstacles and setbacks are inevitable parts of life, but our responses to them significantly impact our growth and success. Through Dr. Wayne Dyer's powerful call to action, "Don't die with your music still inside of you," we understood the importance of unleashing our true potential and sharing our unique contributions with the world. We discussed strategies for overcoming fears, balancing multiple passions, and creating routines that allow us to thrive despite obstacles. The power of writing down our fears was highlighted as a tool for bringing anxieties into the light, examining them, and ultimately overcoming them. By embracing uncertainty and confronting our fears directly, we can reveal our resilience, adaptability, and immense possibilities.

Today, we'll focus on the importance of showing gratitude and using positive affirmations. These practices are essential for maintaining a positive outlook and staying motivated on your journey toward your goals. Gratitude shifts your focus from what you lack to what you have, fostering a sense of abundance and contentment. Positive affirmations help rewire your brain, replacing negative self-talk with empowering beliefs that propel you forward.

As we dive deeper into these practices, we'll explore practical strategies for integrating gratitude and affirmations into your daily life. You'll learn how to create a gratitude journal, develop personalized affirmations, and use these tools to overcome challenges and stay motivated. By the end of this chapter, you'll have a comprehensive toolkit for nurturing a positive mindset and sustaining your motivation on the path to achieving your dreams.

Building a Support System and Cultivating Self-Motivation

As you journey towards your dreams, cultivate relationships with people who believe in your vision and actively encourage you to pursue them. These individuals will uplift you during challenging times, celebrate your successes, and provide constructive feedback when needed. Their positive energy and unwavering support can reignite your passion and remind you of your potential.

Surround yourself with friends, family, mentors, or online communities that share your values and aspirations. Together, you can create a powerful network that propels you towards your goals.

Building a strong support system is crucial, but equally important is cultivating your own inner drive. This is where self-motivation comes in. Remember, the path to your dreams is a marathon, not a sprint. It requires patience, perseverance, and a willingness to embrace challenges. However, with a clear roadmap, unwavering determination, and a wellspring of self-motivation, you can transform your aspirations into tangible accomplishments.

In today's whirlwind of demands and distractions, the practices of gratitude and positive affirmations stand as powerful tools for self-mastery and personal growth. They act as a counterbalance to the negative self-talk that can erode our confidence and cloud our vision.

When we appreciate our blessings and focus on our strengths and goals, we create an environment for personal growth. These practices not only boost our self-esteem but also instill a profound sense of purpose and direction. It allows us to unlock our full potential and manifest a life that aligns with our deepest desires.

The Power of Intention

Several years ago, I stumbled upon Dr. Wayne Dyer's enlightening book, *The Power of Intention*. His words resonated deeply, and I was inspired to create my own personalized affirmations. This might sound a bit unconventional, but it has become a transformative practice for me. Every morning, I take a moment to express my gratitude to God for all the blessings in my life. (Feel free to replace "Father" or "God" with whatever resonates with your personal beliefs and practices.)

> Heavenly Father, my heart overflows with gratitude for the countless blessings you've bestowed upon my life. Thank you for the love, laughter, and warmth that my wife and beautiful children bring into our home. I am grateful for their presence in my life, and for the abundance we enjoy in health and prosperity. I'm eternally grateful for the love and support of my family and friends.
>
> Lord, I humbly ask that you continue to shower your blessings upon my family, keeping us safe and guiding us on your path. Please work through me, using my talents, knowledge, and skills to bring glory to your name. May my hands be your instruments of healing—my words are a source of encouragement—and my actions are a reflection of your love.
>
> Guide me to use the gifts you've given me to uplift others and make a positive impact on the world. In your holy name, I pray. Amen.

Have you listed out and said these things aloud? Now, it's your turn to embark on a journey of gratitude and self-affirmation. Take a moment to connect with your inner self, your higher power, or the universe—whatever resonates with your personal beliefs.

Find a quiet space where you can reflect and write down a heartfelt prayer of gratitude. Express your thanks for the blessings in your life, big and small.

Acknowledge the people who support and love you, the opportunities that have come your way, and the challenges that have shaped you.

Here's a template to get you started. Personalize it and make it your own.

Dear [Your Higher Power/Universe/Inner Self],

My heart overflows with gratitude for the countless blessings you've bestowed upon my life. Thank you for

_____

_____

_____

_____

_____

_____

_____

_____

_____

_____

_____

_____

_____

_____

Fill in the blanks with your own words, expressing your unique appreciation for the gifts you've received. Let your heart guide your pen as you write a prayer that reflects your deepest gratitude and reverence for the abundance in your life.

Following this prayer, I recite my affirmations with passion and conviction. Don't just go through the motions; speak the words as if you already believe them to be true. Feel the emotions behind each affirmation and the excitement of achieving your dreams.

Affirmations

When you speak your affirmations with passion and conviction, you send a powerful message to your subconscious mind. You're not just stating desires; you're declaring your unwavering belief in your ability to achieve them. This belief is a key ingredient in manifesting your dreams into reality.

Remember, your affirmations are not mere words; they are seeds of intention that you plant in the fertile ground of your mind. When you nurture them with passion and conviction, you create a fertile environment for growth and transformation. These carefully crafted statements embody my aspirations, reminding me of my strengths and potential.

> I am healthy, attracting abundance in all forms. I am a scholar, destined to earn my doctorate degree. My dream job awaits me, a perfect match for my talents and passions. I am a gifted writer, sharing my stories with the world. I am a homeowner and love living in my hometown. I am a devoted husband and father, nurturing a legacy of love and laughter. I am a loyal friend, always present and supportive. I am a valuable member of my community, making a positive impact through my actions. I am grateful for the blessing and excited about the future that unfolds before me.

It's a daily ritual that sets a positive tone for the day ahead, reinforcing my belief in myself and my goals. While it might seem a tad eccentric, this practice has proven to be incredibly empowering. By starting each day with gratitude and affirmations, I cultivate a mindset of abundance and possibility.

I invite you to experiment with this approach, tailoring it to your own beliefs and aspirations. Remember, the power of positive affirmations lies in their consistent repetition. Make it a daily habit to say these empowering words to yourself, watch as your mindset shifts, and see your actions align with your deepest desires.

In a society that often bombards us with negative messages and unrealistic expectations, affirmations provide a powerful antidote. They remind us of our inherent worth, our potential for greatness, and our ability to overcome challenges. By intentionally choosing positive affirmations, we can create a more empowering narrative for ourselves and ultimately shape our reality for the better.

In conclusion, affirmations, though not always explicitly named, are deeply ingrained in various religious and spiritual traditions. They serve as tools for cultivating a positive mindset, aligning with divine principles, and manifesting desired outcomes. Whether through prayer, mantras, scripture verses, or personal declarations, the power of positive words to shape our beliefs and actions is universally recognized and embraced.

John's Gratitude Practice: Transforming Life with Positive Affirmations

John, a successful project manager, often felt overwhelmed by the pressures of his job. Despite his accomplishments, he felt constantly stressed and unfulfilled. One evening, after a particularly challenging day at work, he confided in his close friend, Janet.

"Janet, I'm feeling really burned out," John sighed, his voice heavy with exhaustion. "I've achieved a lot in my career, but I still feel stressed and unsatisfied. It's like I'm always chasing something, but I don't know what."

Janet nodded empathetically, "I understand, John. It's easy to get caught up in the hustle and lose sight of what's truly important. Have you ever tried incorporating gratitude and positive affirmations into your daily routine?"

John looked skeptical, "Gratitude? Positive affirmations? I've heard of them, but I'm not sure how they could help."

Janet smiled warmly, "They can make a huge difference, John. By focusing on what you're grateful for and affirming positive aspects of your life, you can shift your mindset and reduce stress. Let's start with some simple steps."

Starting a Gratitude Practice
Janet suggested that John start a gratitude journal, writing down three things he was grateful for each day. She also encouraged him to use positive affirmations to reinforce a positive mindset.

"Every evening, take a few minutes to write down three things you're grateful for," Janet instructed. "It could be anything—big or small. Also, try repeating positive affirmations each morning. For example, 'I am capable and strong,' or 'I am grateful for the opportunities today will bring.'"

John agreed, "Okay, I'll give it a try. It sounds simple enough."

Finding the Positives
As the weeks went by, John diligently wrote in his gratitude journal and recited his affirmations each morning. He began to notice subtle but significant changes in his outlook and mood. The practice of focusing on positive aspects of his day helped him appreciate the little things and reduced his overall stress. He began to realize how lucky he was to have a supportive friend like Janet, a comfortable home, and a job that challenged him.

Deepening the Practice

Encouraged by the positive changes, John decided to deepen his gratitude practice. He started sharing his gratitude with others, expressing appreciation to his colleagues, friends, and family for their support, kindness, and contributions to his life. This not only strengthened his relationships but also reinforced his own sense of gratitude. He made it a point to tell his wife how much he appreciated her cooking or to thank a colleague for their help on a project.

Overcoming Challenges

There were days when John struggled to find things to be grateful for, especially during tough times at work. On those days, Janet reminded him to focus on even the smallest positives and use his affirmations to stay grounded. When John was feeling overwhelmed by a deadline, Janet reminded him of his past successes and encouraged him to repeat his affirmations.

Over time, John's gratitude practice became a natural part of his daily routine. He felt more content, resilient, and connected to the people around him. The stress that once dominated his life was now manageable, and he found joy in the present moment. He realized that gratitude and positive affirmations had not only changed his mindset but also improved his overall well-being.

Conclusion

Today, we've explored the transformative power of gratitude and positive affirmations in maintaining a positive mindset and sustaining motivation. By focusing on what we are grateful for and reinforcing positive beliefs about ourselves, we can build resilience, enhance our well-being, and stay motivated on our journey toward our goals. These practices not only help us overcome challenges but also foster a sense of fulfillment and joy in our daily lives.

As you continue to incorporate gratitude and positive affirmations into your routine, remember that consistency is key. Make these practices a regular part of your day, and observe how they gradually transform your outlook and boost your motivation. Celebrate your progress, no matter how small, and keep nurturing the positive mindset that fuels your drive.

Tomorrow, we will embark on the last day of our 17-day journey. We will reflect on the progress you've made, the lessons you've learned, and the new habits you've cultivated. Get ready to embrace your power, shape your destiny, and take the next steps on your self-motivation journey. Together, we will celebrate your achievements and set the stage for continued growth and success.

"Anyone who stops learning is old, whether at twenty or eighty. Anyone who keeps learning stays young."

—Henry Ford

DAY 17:

EMBRACING YOUR POWER: A NEW CHAPTER OF SELF-MOTIVATION

Congratulations on completing the 17-Day Dream Blueprint! Over the past 17 days, you've embarked on a transformative journey of self-discovery, motivation, and growth. You've unearthed your dreams, broadened your horizons, embraced challenges, built a supportive network, charted your course with SMART goals, and mastered resilience in the face of setbacks. Each day has equipped you with invaluable insights and tools to Define, Reimagine, Embrace, Assemble, Map, and ACT to turn your dreams into reality.

As you step into this new chapter, remember that the power to shape your destiny lies within you. Embrace your power, trust in your abilities, and continue to cultivate the habits and mindsets that will drive your success. The end of this blueprint is just the beginning of your ongoing journey toward a fulfilling and purpose-driven life.

Interactive Reflection

Tomorrow, as you wake up, carry forward the lessons and practices you've learned. Continue to set ambitious goals, maintain your motivation, and surround yourself with positivity and support. Reflect on your progress regularly, celebrate your achievements, and never stop striving for your dreams. Your future is bright, and your potential is limitless. Embrace it with unwavering confidence and enthusiasm.

Thank you for allowing me to be a part of your journey. Here's to your continued success and the realization of your most cherished dreams.

Reflecting on Your Journey of Self-Motivation

Throughout our journey, we have explored the multifaceted landscape of self-motivation, uncovering its origins, dissecting its science, and learning how to cultivate it through the ACT method to empower our lives:

- **Align**: We've distinguished between intrinsic and extrinsic motivation, recognizing the importance of aligning our actions with our values and passions for lasting fulfillment.
- **Cultivate**: We've learned to cultivate supportive environments, build self-efficacy, and harness the power of habit to propel ourselves toward our goals.
- **Transform**: We've explored the transformative power of passion, faced our roadblocks head-on, and tapped into the flow state to experience joy and engagement in our pursuits.

Your Next Steps on the Journey

Now, it's time to take the reins and continue to DRIVE your destiny with self-motivation:

- Direction: What new, challenging goals aligned with your values will you set? Write down at least three goals.

Goal 1: _____

Goal 2: _____

Goal 3: _____

- Resilience: What challenges do you anticipate, and how will you embrace them as steppingstones? Reflect on past challenges and how you overcame them.

Challenges: _____

Steppingstones: _____

- Inspiration: Who will you share your journey with to inspire others? Will you reach out to friends, family, or colleagues?

People to Inspire: _____

- Victory: What recent successes, big or small, will you celebrate, and how will you celebrate them?

Successes: _____

Celebration Plans: _____

- Evaluate: How will you regularly reflect on your progress, refine your approach, and continue your growth?

Reflection Plan: _____

Conclusion and Introduction to Lifelong Learning

Remember, self-motivation is not a destination but a lifelong journey of growth and self-discovery. By embracing your inner power and continually applying the DREAM and ACTDRIVE methods, you can unleash your full potential, create the life you desire, and leave a lasting legacy. The journey continues. Embrace your power, shape your destiny, and become the best version of yourself. The journey begins now.

Final Conclusion and Looking Ahead

Today marks the culmination of an incredible journey through the 17-Day Dream Blueprint. You've gained invaluable tools and insights to fuel your motivation, achieve your goals, and live a fulfilling life. But this is just the beginning. As you move forward, continue to embrace challenges, nurture your growth, and celebrate your successes.

Tomorrow, and every day after, is an opportunity to apply what you've learned. Stay curious, keep learning, and remain committed to your dreams.

Remember, the power to shape your destiny lies within you. Keep moving forward with confidence and determination.

Thank you for allowing me to be a part of your journey. Here's to your continued success and the realization of your most cherished dreams. Now, go forth and conquer—your future awaits!

Notes

BIBLIOGRAPHY

Alblooshi, Mohamed, Mohammad Shamsuzzaman, and Salah Haridy. "The Relationship between Leadership Styles and Organisational Innovation." *European Journal of Innovation Management* 24, no. 2 (2020): 338–70. https://doi.org/10.1108/ejim-11-2019-0339.

Aljumah, Abdulsalam. "The Impact of Extrinsic and Intrinsic Motivation on Job Satisfaction: The Mediating Role of Transactional Leadership." *Cogent Business and Management* 10, no. 3 (2023). https://doi.org/10.1080/23311975.2023.2270813.

Bartlett, Larissa, Marie-Jeanne Buscot, Aidan Bindoff, Richard Chambers, and Craig Hassed. "Mindfulness Is Associated with Lower Stress and Higher Work Engagement in a Large Sample of Mooc Participants." *Frontiers in Psychology* 12 (2021). https://doi.org/10.3389/fpsyg.2021.724126.

Bjerke, May Britt, and Ralph Renger. "Being Smart About Writing Smart Objectives." *Evaluation and Program Planning* 61 (2017): 125–27. https://doi.org/10.1016/j.evalprogplan.2016.12.009.

Brown, Les . "The Graveyard Is the Richest Place on Earth." Accessed June 6, 2024. https://www.youtube.com/watch?v=YgjNfn8nlj8.

Carden, Lucas, and Wendy Wood. "Habit Formation and Change." *Current Opinion in Behavioral Sciences* 20 (2018): 117–22. https://doi.org/10.1016/j.cobeha.2017.12.009.

Dyer, Serena J. J. and Wayne W. Dyer. *Don't Die with Your Music Still in You: My Experience Growing Up with Spiritual Parents*. First edition. N.p.: Hay House, 2014.

Ferreira-Neto, Macário Neri, Jessyca Lages de Carvalho Castro, José Milton de Sousa-Filho, and Bruno de Souza Lessa. "The Role of Self-Efficacy, Entrepreneurial Passion, and Creativity in Developing Entrepreneurial Intentions." *Frontiers in Psychology* 14 (2023). https://doi.org/10.3389/fpsyg.2023.1134618.

Grassinger, Robert, Monique Landberg, Sami Määttä, Kati Vasalampi, and Sonja Bieg. "Interplay of Intrinsic Motivation and Well-Being at School." *Motivation and Emotion* 48, no. 2 (2024): 147–54. https://doi.org/10.1007/s11031-024-10057-2.

Holiday, Ryan. *The Obstacle Is the Way: The Timeless Art of Turning Trials into Triumph*. 1st ed. N.p.: Portfolio, 2014.

Kristensen, Sara Madeleine, Torill Marie Bogsnes Larsen, Helga Bjørnøy Urke, and Anne Grete Danielsen. "Academic Stress, Academic Self-Efficacy, and Psychological Distress: A Moderated Mediation of Within-Person Effects." *Journal of Youth and Adolescence* 52, no. 7 (2023): 1512–29. https://doi.org/10.1007/s10964-023-01770-1.

Linge, Anita Dyb, Stål Kapstø Bjørkly, Chris Jensen, and Bente Hasle. "Bandura's Self-Efficacy Model Used to Explore Participants' Experiences of Health, Lifestyle, and Work After Attending a Vocational Rehabilitation Program with Lifestyle Intervention – a Focus Group Study." *Journal of Multidisciplinary Healthcare* Volume 14 (2021): 3533–48. https://doi.org/10.2147/jmdh.s334620.

"Bandura's Self-Efficacy Model Used to Explore Participants' Experiences of Health, Lifestyle, and Work After Attending a Vocational Rehabilitation Program with Lifestyle Intervention – a Focus Group Study." *Journal of Multidisciplinary Healthcare* Volume 14 (2021): 3533–48. https://doi.org/10.2147/jmdh.s334620.

Liu, Yuxia, Yang Yang, Xue Bai, Yujie Chen, and Lei Mo. "Do Immediate External Rewards Really Enhance Intrinsic Motivation?" *Frontiers in Psychology* 13 (2022). https://doi.org/10.3389/fpsyg.2022.853879.

Mercader-Rubio, Isabel, Nieves Gutiérrez Ángel, Sofia Silva, Guilherme Furtado, and Sónia Brito-Costa. "Intrinsic Motivation: Knowledge, Achievement, and Experimentation in Sports Science Students—relations with Emotional Intelligence." *Behavioral Sciences* 13, no. 7 (2023): 589. https://doi.org/10.3390/bs13070589.

Ng, Betsy. "The Neuroscience of Growth Mindset and Intrinsic Motivation." *Brain Sciences* 8, no. 2 (2018): 20. https://doi.org/10.3390/brainsci8020020.

Peifer, Corinna, Gina Wolters, László Harmat, Jean Heutte, Jasmine Tan, Teresa Freire, Dionísia Tavares, Carla Fonte, Frans Orsted Andersen, Jef van den Hout, Milija Šimleša, Linda Pola, Lucia Ceja, and Stefano Triberti. "A Scoping Review of Flow Research." *Frontiers in Psychology* 13 (2022). https://doi.org/10.3389/fpsyg.2022.815665.

Pincus, J. David. "The Structure of Human Motivation." *BMC Psychology* 11, no. 1 (2023). https://doi.org/10.1186/s40359-023-01346-5.

Review, Harvard Business. *Hbr's 10 Must Reads on Emotional Intelligence (with Featured Article "What Makes a Leader?" by Daniel Goleman) (hbr's 10 Must Reads)*. 1st ed. N.p.: Harvard Business Review Press, 2015.

"The Relationship of Academic Self-Efficacy, Goal Orientation, and Personal Goal Setting Among High School Students." *Frontiers in Educational Research* 4, no. 11 (2021). https://doi.org/10.25236/fer.2021.041109.

Urhahne, Detlef, and Lisette Wijnia. "Theories of Motivation in Education: An Integrative Framework." *Educational Psychology Review* 35, no. 2 (2023). https://doi.org/10.1007/s10648-023-09767-9.

Wang, Heqiao, and Gary A. Troia. "How Students' Writing Motivation, Teachers' Personal and Professional Attributes, and Writing Instruction Impact Student Writing Achievement: A Two-Level Hierarchical Linear Modeling Study." *Frontiers in Psychology* 14 (2023). https://doi.org/10.3389/fpsyg.2023.1213929.

Xue, Hanbing, Yifei Luo, Yuxiang Luan, and Nan Wang. "A Meta-Analysis of Leadership and Intrinsic Motivation: Examining Relative Importance and Moderators." *Frontiers in Psychology* 13 (2022). https://doi.org/10.3389/fpsyg.2022.941161.

INDEX

A

ACTDRIVE method 16, 19, 37, 219

Affirmations 21, 21–236, 38, 38–236, 63, 63–236, 105, 105–236, 106, 106–236, 204, 204–236, 204–236, 207, 207–236, 207–236, 207–236, 207–236, 208, 208–236, 209, 209–236, 211, 211–236, 211–236, 211–236, 212, 212–236, 212–236, 212–236, 212–236, 212–236, 213, 213–236, 213–236, 213–236, 213–236, 213–236, 214–236, 215–236

Anna's Fitness Routine 121

B

Building Self-Efficacy 61

C

Carlos's Leadership Journey 156

Challenges 5, 6, 7, 8, 16, 20, 27, 32, 33, 38, 39, 43, 53, 63, 64, 67, 70, 80, 89, 91, 94, 99, 103, 105, 111, 120, 127, 131, 132, 134, 135, 137, 138, 141, 149, 151, 153, 154, 157, 188, 189, 193, 194, 197, 203, 204, 207, 208, 210, 212, 214, 217, 218, 229, 233

Charting Your Course 24

Chris's Artistic Flow 82

Community 31, 32, 33, 58, 111, 112, 187, 188, 200, 211

Confidence 6, 7, 10, 11, 16, 32, 34, 38, 41, 42, 59, 61, 62, 63, 68, 69, 70, 76, 89, 98, 104, 105, 116, 136, 199, 208, 217, 220

Creating Your Personal Haven 164

Cultivating Gratitude 76, 77

Cultivating Self-Motivation 149, 208

D

Define your dreams 1
Discipline 30, 38, 130, 192

E

Elena's Connection Quest 143
Embrace challenges 30, 42, 85, 208, 219
Embracing 2, 84, 103, 104, 127, 141, 189, 194, 197, 203, 207, 219
Environmental influences 34, 43, 47
Extrinsic motivation 44, 47, 49, 50, 58, 218

F

Finding balance 197
Finding Flow 83
Finding Joy 56, 82, 202
First step 2, 5, 9, 12, 13, 20, 31, 33, 41, 116, 127, 175, 199

G

Goal Setting 27, 61, 226
Gratitude Practice 135, 212, 213

H

Habit Formation 7, 174, 224
Harnessing Visual Tools 27
Hope 12, 228

I

Inner drive 34, 44, 50, 55, 142, 208
Intrinsic Motivation 38, 47, 48, 49, 50, 149, 223, 224, 225, 226

J

Jake's Home Office Transformation 168

L

Leadership 149, 151, 154, 156, 223, 226, 229
Liam's Music Passion 56
Lifelong learning 179, 183, 189, 194, 197

M

Map out your path 1

Mastery Experiences 62

Maya's Entrepreneurial Journey 135

Michael's Journey to Freedom 174

Mind Maps 27

Motivation 1, 2, 6, 20, 24, 25, 34, 37, 38, 39, 40, 42, 43, 44, 47, 48, 49, 50, 54, 55, 58, 61, 63, 64, 71, 74, 76, 77, 80, 85, 89, 90, 99, 103, 105, 106, 107, 109, 110, 111, 113, 118, 121, 124, 127, 138, 141, 143, 146, 149, 154, 156, 158, 159, 163, 168, 171, 173, 174, 176, 178, 179, 183, 187, 189, 191, 192, 193, 194, 197, 204, 208, 214, 215, 217, 218, 219, 229

N

Next steps 215

O

Overcoming obstacles 104, 128, 141, 194, 233

Overcoming Setbacks 192

P

Path 1, 5, 6, 7, 8, 12, 16, 19, 20, 24, 28, 44, 47, 50, 54, 64, 94, 99, 103, 111, 113, 116, 127, 132, 135, 173, 194, 198, 199, 208, 209, 229

Peak performance 71, 74, 76, 84, 89

Personal Change 20

Personal growth 7, 48, 58, 67, 80, 89, 99, 183, 187, 188, 189, 197, 208

Positivity 146, 217

Power 11, 21, 33, 34, 43, 44, 59, 63, 67, 70, 71, 73, 84, 89, 99, 123, 124, 155, 158, 171, 173, 175, 176, 178, 179, 183, 194, 197, 198, 199, 203, 204, 207, 209, 212, 214, 215, 217, 218, 219, 220, 229, 230

Power of Intention 209

Purpose 9, 19, 28, 40, 48, 64, 67, 74, 75, 76, 85, 89, 90, 95, 99, 103, 118, 119, 121, 153, 154, 164, 188, 189, 206, 208, 217

R

Rachel's Public Speaking 67
Ripple Effect 128, 141, 143
Roadblocks to Resolve 103

S

Sarah's Bookstore Dream 30
Self-Care 39
self-discovery 5, 6, 19, 21, 23, 37, 64, 67, 76, 143, 154, 217, 219, 233
Self-Efficacy 7, 40, 61, 62, 63, 224, 225, 226
Self-Motivation 37, 38, 141, 143, 149, 156, 183, 189, 208, 217, 218
Showing Gratitude 207
SMART goals 16, 24, 25, 26, 33, 37, 110, 111, 217
strengthening relationships 77, 138, 145

T

Taking action 19, 128, 199, 200

V

Values 21, 25, 26, 29, 40, 44, 50, 51, 52, 58, 61, 64, 90, 94, 96, 98, 99, 103, 108, 111, 118, 119, 121, 143, 154, 188, 208, 218
Vicarious Experiences 62

LET'S STAY IN TOUCH!

Dear Reader,

Thank you for joining me on this journey. I hope the stories and insights shared within have resonated with you.

I invite you to continue our dialogue. If you have questions, feedback, or would like to discuss potential collaborations, please contact me at dondi.day@emeraldislepublishing.com. I am also available for speaking engagements and book signings.

For traditional mail correspondence, please use the following address:
P.O. Box 5041
Emerald Isle, NC 28594-5041

If you enjoyed the book, leaving a review on Goodreads.com or Amazon.com would help others discover it. Thank you for your support!

I look forward to hearing from you, and I hope our paths cross again soon.

Sincerely,

Dondi M. Day

PS. You can find me on LinkedIn @ https://www.linkedin.com/in/dondimday/ or on the book of faces @ https://www.facebook.com/profile.php?id=61560913719838

ABOUT THE AUTHOR

Dr. Dondi M. Day is a passionate educator and a seasoned professional. His journey from humble beginnings to a successful career was fueled by an unwavering belief in the power of self-motivation and the transformative potential of education. It's a journey he intimately understands, having walked the path himself and witnessed firsthand the incredible impact it can have. Now armed with a Doctor of Business Administration (DBA) degree in Leadership from Liberty University, he is driven to share his knowledge and experience to empower others to achieve their own dreams.

Dr. Day's passion for teaching shines through in his interactions with the over 5,000 project management professionals he has mentored for over a decade. He is not just a consultant; he's a guide, helping others navigate the challenges of their careers and personal lives. His expertise is sought after by leading Fortune Global 500 companies, where he has consistently delivered exceptional results. Dr. Day's unique blend of practical experience and academic rigor is evident in his authorship. He has penned "The Practical Guide to Contracts & Other Essential Knowledge," a go-to resource for professionals in the field, and he has also ventured into fiction with "Calico Creek: A Quest for Pirate's Treasure" and "Calico Creek: The Howling Marauder and the Pirate's Secret." These stories, like his life, are a testament to the power of dreams and the resilience of the human spirit.

ADDITIONAL PUBLISHED WORKS

The Practical Guide to Contracts & Other Essential Knowledge: What They Are Teaching Executives and Project Managers.

Genre: Nonfiction, Self-help

About: The book is a comprehensive guidebook designed to help individuals at all levels within an organization understand and navigate the complexities of contracts. Day, a seasoned contracts and construction claims manager, shares his expertise and experiences in a user-friendly, conversational style, making the book accessible to both newcomers and seasoned professionals in project management.

The guidebook delves into the intricacies of contract formation, terms and conditions, change orders, disputes, and construction claims management. It offers practical, hands-on knowledge and tools that can be readily applied in real-world scenarios. Through a series of relatable stories and examples, Day guides readers through the pitfalls commonly encountered in projects, equipping them with the skills and knowledge to mitigate risks and successfully complete their jobs. Whether you are new to project management or a seasoned professional, this guidebook is a valuable resource for anyone looking to enhance their understanding of contracts and improve their project management skills.

Calico Creek: A Quests for Pirates Treasure

Genre: Fiction, Young Adult

About: Fourteen-year-old Michael Dondi Smythwick and his friends are bored. School is out for the summer, and it's hot in their small town of Morehead City, North Carolina. Dondi and his friends spend their days fishing, crabbing, and building a fort in the woods. One day, Dondi's mother shares a secret about their family history. She reveals that Dondi was named after his great-great-grandfather, Jonathan, a pirate who sailed the seas in the 1700s. Dondi and his friends are captivated by the story and set out to uncover the truth about Jonathan's past.

Their quest for answers leads them on an adventure filled with twists and turns. They discover a hidden root cellar, a mysterious map, and a treasure chest filled with gold coins. Along the way, they learn about the history of piracy in North Carolina and the importance of friendship and family. Dondi and his friends must use their wits and courage to uncover the truth about Jonathan's past and the treasure he left behind.

Calico Creek: The Legend of Shadow's Marauder and the Pirate's Secret

Genre: Fiction, Young Adult

About: This book features a strong female character, Aisling Thorne, who defies traditional gender roles and excels in a male-dominated field. Aisling is a skilled shipwright who is not afraid to get her hands dirty and prove her worth. She is also intelligent, resourceful, and brave. She is a positive role model for young girls who want to see themselves represented in adventurous stories.

The book also promotes themes of leadership, empowerment, perseverance, and the importance of following one's dreams. Aisling's journey is one of self-discovery and overcoming obstacles. She learns to trust her instincts, stand up for herself, and never give up on her goals. These are all valuable lessons for young girls who are navigating the challenges of adolescence and young adulthood.

www.ingramcontent.com/pod-product-compliance
Lightning Source LLC
Chambersburg PA
CBHW050252010526
44107CB00003B/294